Selected Plates from the Classic
"Le Fontane di Roma," 1660-1675

The Fountains of
ROME

GIOVANNI BATTISTA FALDA
and GIOVANNI FRANCESCO VENTURINI

Dover Publications, Inc.
Mineola, New York

PUBLISHER'S NOTE

Born in Valduggia, Italy, it was apparent that Giovanni Battista Falda (c. 1640–1678) had a talent for drawing at a very young age. At fourteen, he was apprenticed to a local painter, and later that same year he was sent to Rome to study under Gian Lorenzo Bernini. He was discovered by Giacomo de Rossi, the son of the founder of the most successful Italian printing press of the time, and trained as an architectural engraver. With the support of de Rossi, Falda enjoyed moderate success as an architect, artist, and engraver, and created his two classic works, *Palazzi di Roma* (Places of Rome) and books one and two of *Le fontane di Roma* (Fountains of Rome), as well as a detailed, twelve-plate map of Rome, and a number of works featuring gardens, and public and religious ceremonies.

It was during the second half of the seventeenth century that it became popular for young, upper-class European men to travel through Italy and France in pursuit of art and culture. It was thanks to these "Grand Tour" participants that Falda's career began to flourish. Frequently commissioned to create images of landmarks for tourists to keep as mementos of Rome, the artist enjoyed a comfortable life until his death in 1678.

Giovanni Francesco Venturini (1650–c. 1710) was born in Rome, and is credited with books three and four of *Le fontane di Roma.* His meticulous accuracy gives way to speculation that he may have been a pupil of Giovanni Battista Galestruzzi, but sadly, little else about Venturini's life is known.

This book contains a selection of plates from the masterpiece *Le fontane di Roma,* widely considered to contain some of the finest and most accurate drawings of the Italian baroque period. Of interest to Roman or architectural history enthusiasts, as well as art lovers and travelers, the images incorporate the surrounding landscape or cityscape, as well as people engaged in the traditional recreational activities of the time.

Bibliographical Note
The Fountains of Rome—Selected Plates from the Classic "Le Fontane di Roma," 1660–1675, first published by Dover Publications, Inc., contains a selection of plates from *Le Fontane di Rome Nelle Piazze e Luoghi Pubblici Della Città.* Rome: Giacomo de Rossi, n.d. [c. 1691]. Marco Natoli has provided the English translations of the captions.

International Standard Book Number
ISBN-13: 978-0-486-49385-5
ISBN-10: 0-486-49385-7

Manufactured in the United States by Courier Corporation
49385701   2014
www.doverpublications.com

LE FONTANE DI ROMA

NELLE PIAZZE,

E LVOGHI PVBLICI DELLA CITTÀ,

CON LI LORO PROSPETTI,

COME SONO AL PRESENTE.

DISEGNATE, ET INTAGLIATE

DA GIO: BATTISTA FALDA.

Date in luce con direttione, e cura da GIO: GIACOMO DE ROSSI, dalle sue stampe in Roma alla Pace con Priu. del S. Pont.

LIBRO PRIMO.

FOUNTAINS OF ROME, IN PIAZZAS AND OTHER PUBLIC PLACES OF THE CITY, AND THEIR FRONTAL VIEWS AS THEY LOOK AT THE PRESENT TIME. DRAWN AND ENGRAVED BY GIO. BATTISTA FALDA. PRINTED, SUPERVISED, AND EDITED BY GIO. GIACOMO DE ROSSI FOR HIS PRESS IN VIA DELLA PACE IN ROME AND WITH THE PATRONAGE OF THE HOLY FATHER. BOOK ONE.

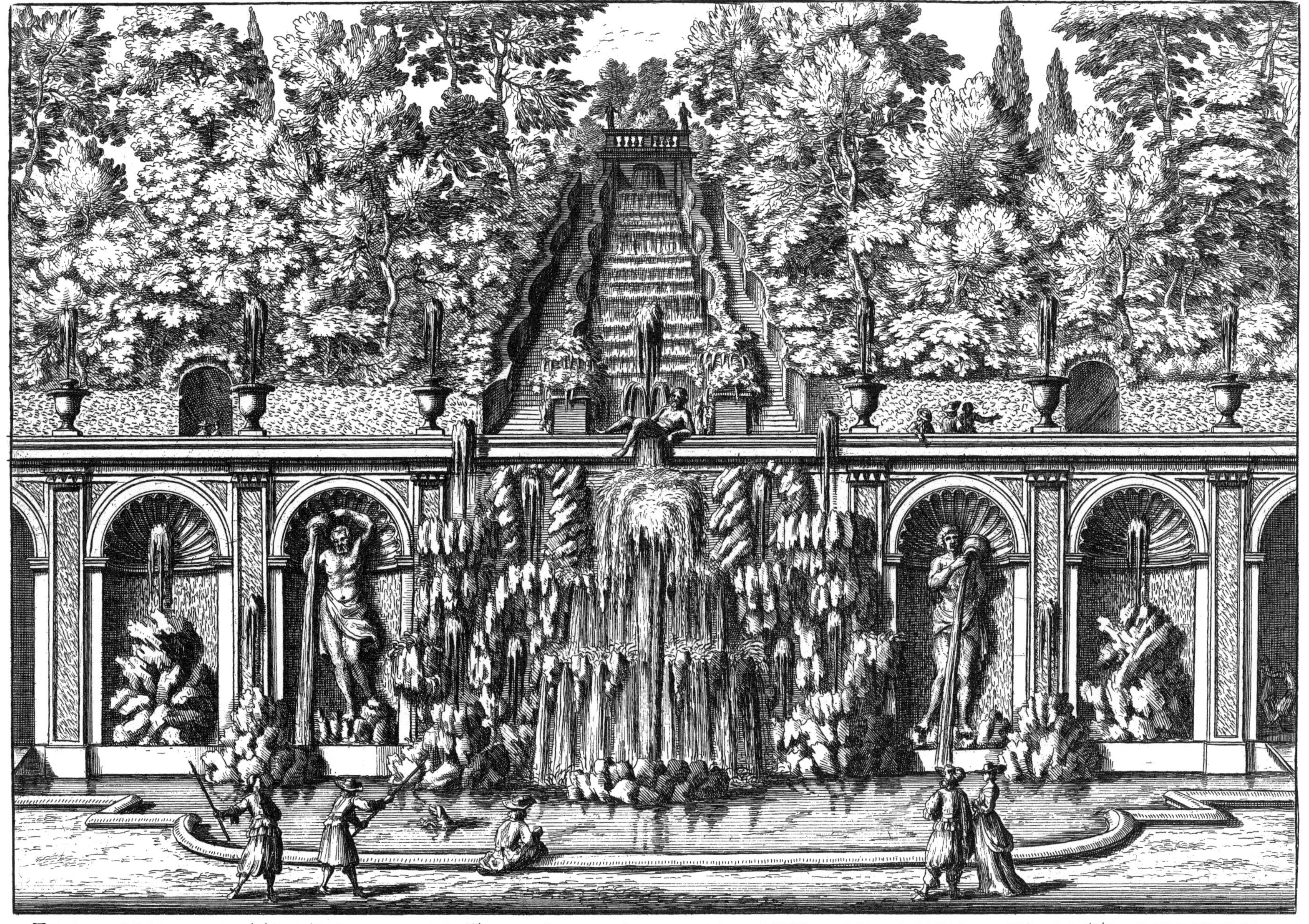

PROSPETTO DEL TEATRO, E CASCATA DELL ACQVE DELLA VILLA LVDOVISIA A FRASCATI CON VARII GIVOCHI D' ACQVE.

FRONTAL VIEW OF THE THEATER, AND WATERFALLS OF VILLA LUDOVISIA IN FRASCATI WITH VARIOUS WATERWORKS.

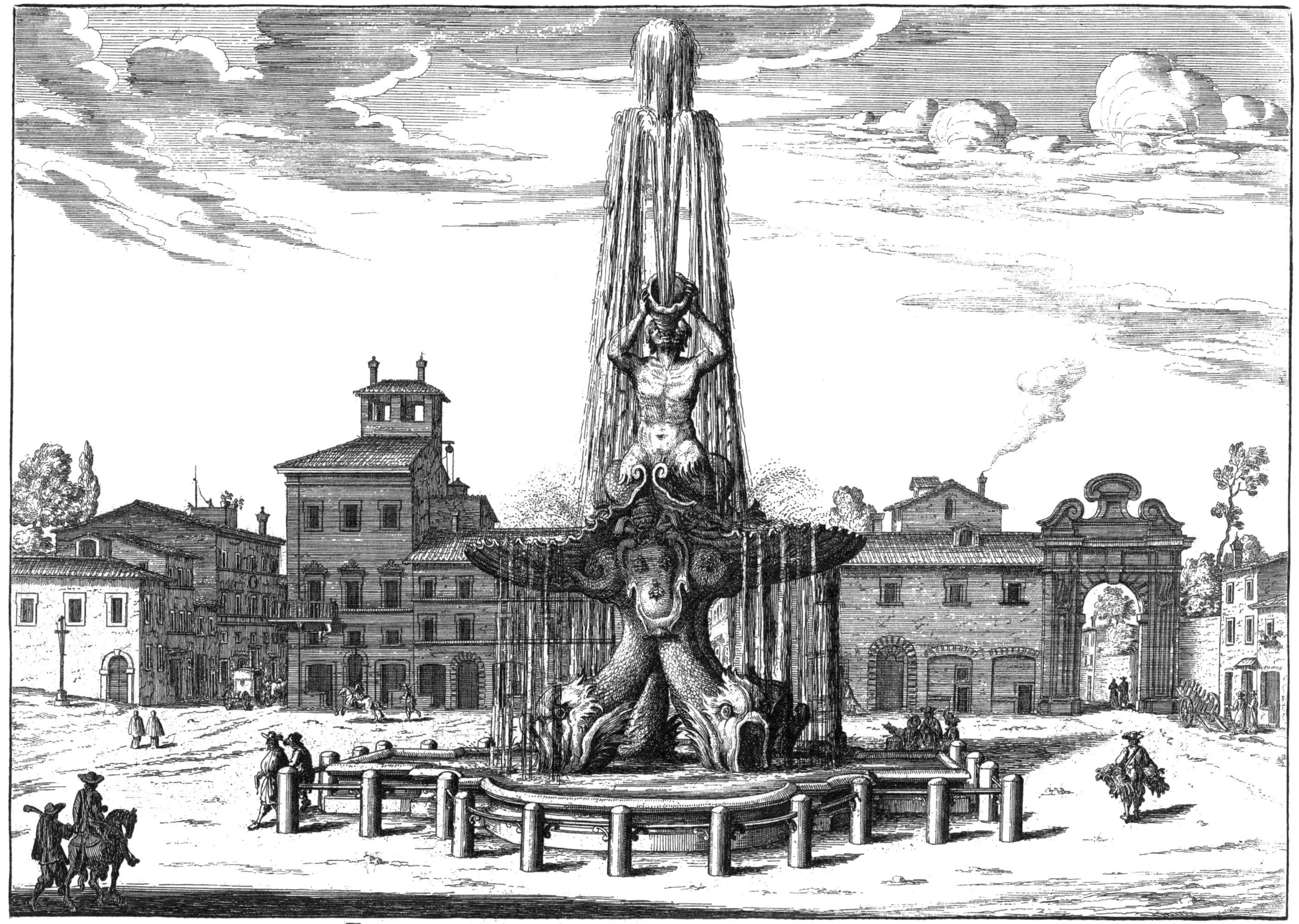

Fontana del Sig. Prencipe di Pallestrina

sù la Piazza Barberina, alle radici del Quirinale in Via felice, nel Rione di Treui, Architet.ᵃ del Cau. Gio. Lorenzo Bernini.

FOUNTAIN OF THE PRINCE OF PALESTRINA, IN PIAZZA BARBERINI AT THE FOOT OF THE QUIRINAL HILL IN THE TREVI DISTRICT. ARCHITECTURE BY SIR GIO. LORENZO BERNINI.

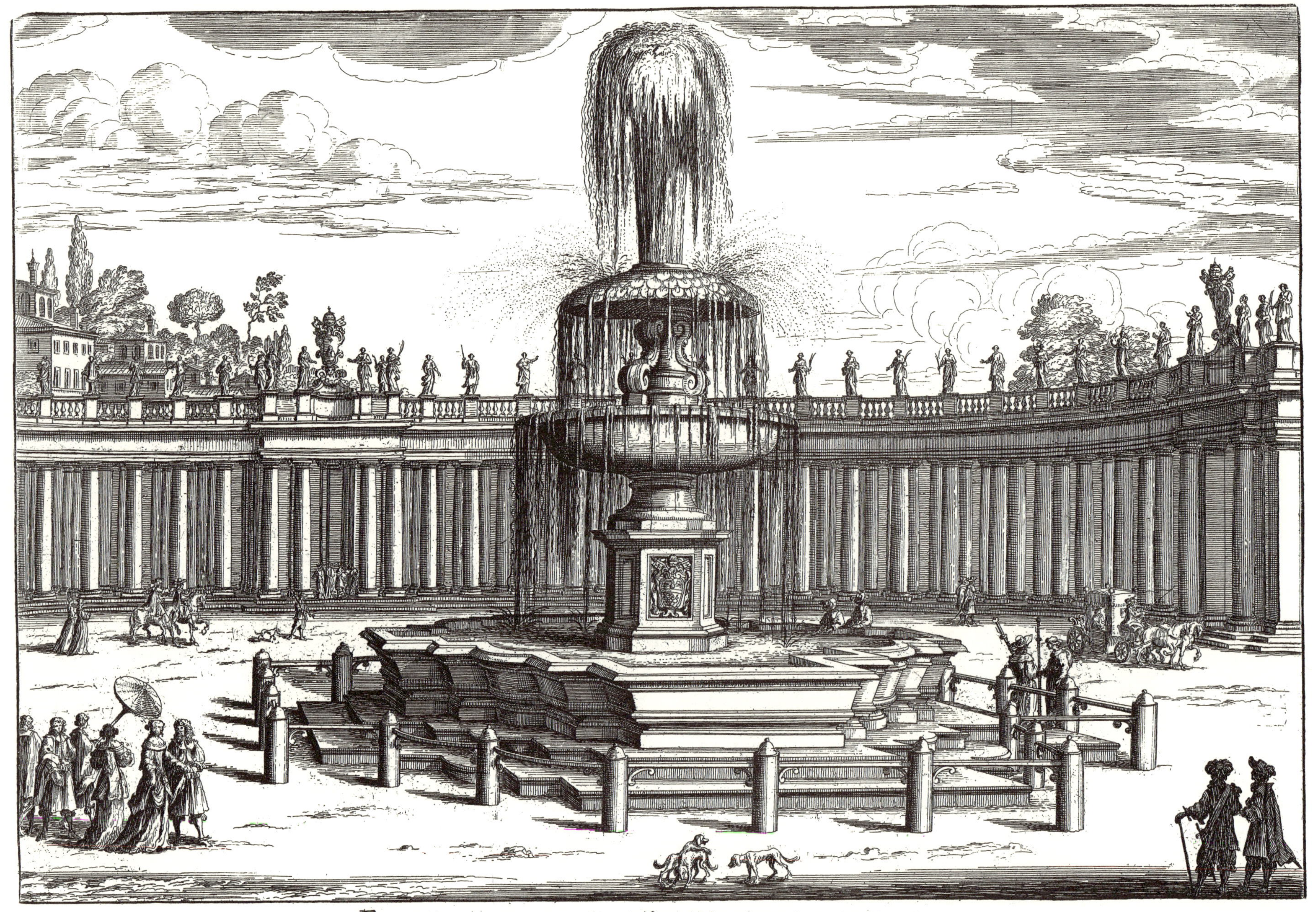

FONTANA DOPPIA NE' LATI DELLA GVGLIA,

nella Piazza, e Portici della Basilica Vaticana, Architet.[a] del Cau.[e] Carlo Maderno.

TWIN FOUNTAIN IN THE PIAZZA BESIDE THE OBELISK, AND COLONNADE OF THE VATICAN BASILICA.
ARCHITECTURE BY SIR CARLO MADERNO.

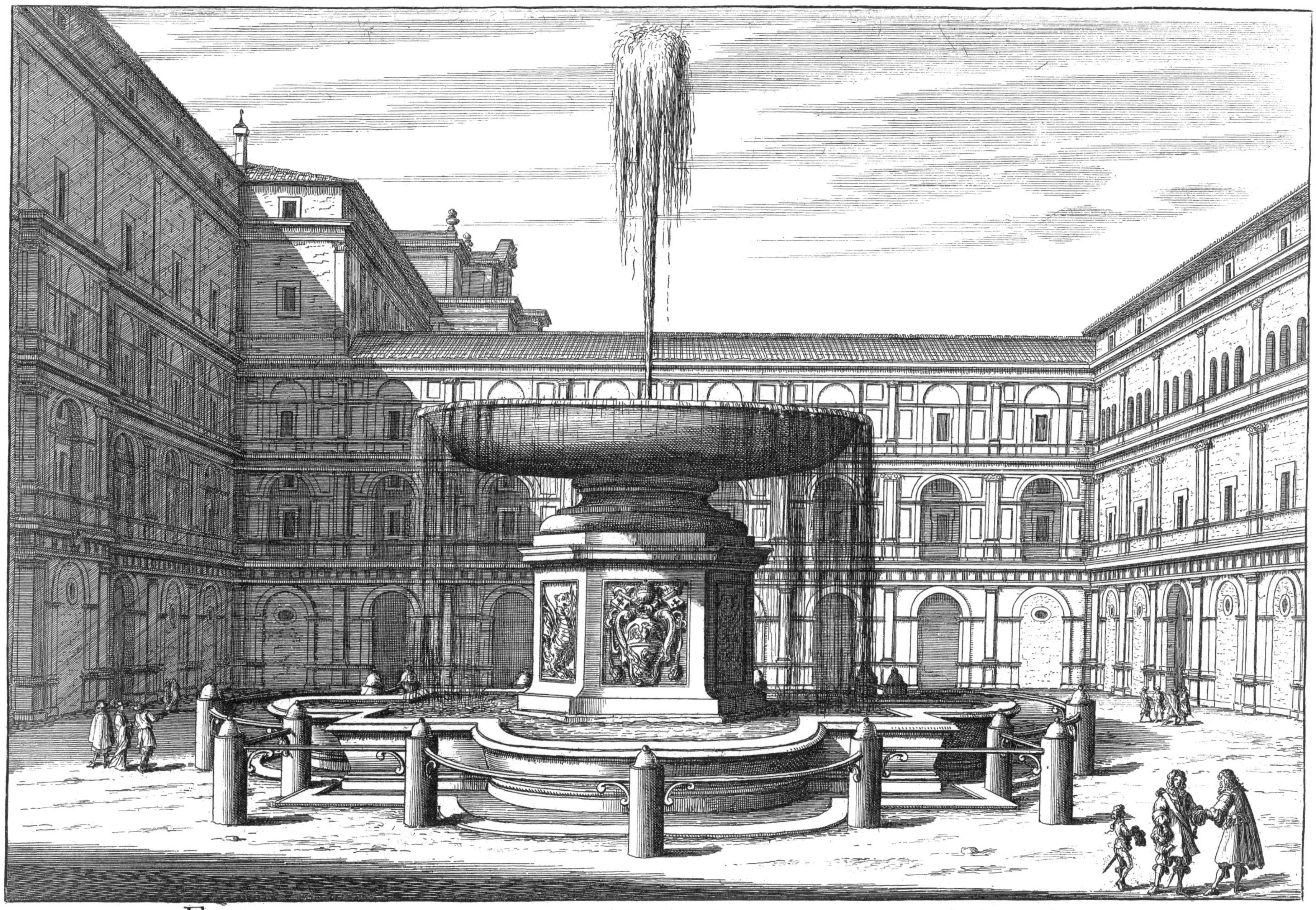

FONTANA NEL GRAN CORTILE DEL PALAZZO VATICANO

detto Belvedere, Architettura di Carlo Maderno.

VATICAN PALACE, FOUNTAIN IN THE COURTYARD KNOWN AS BELVEDERE. ARCHITECTURE BY CARLO MADERNO.

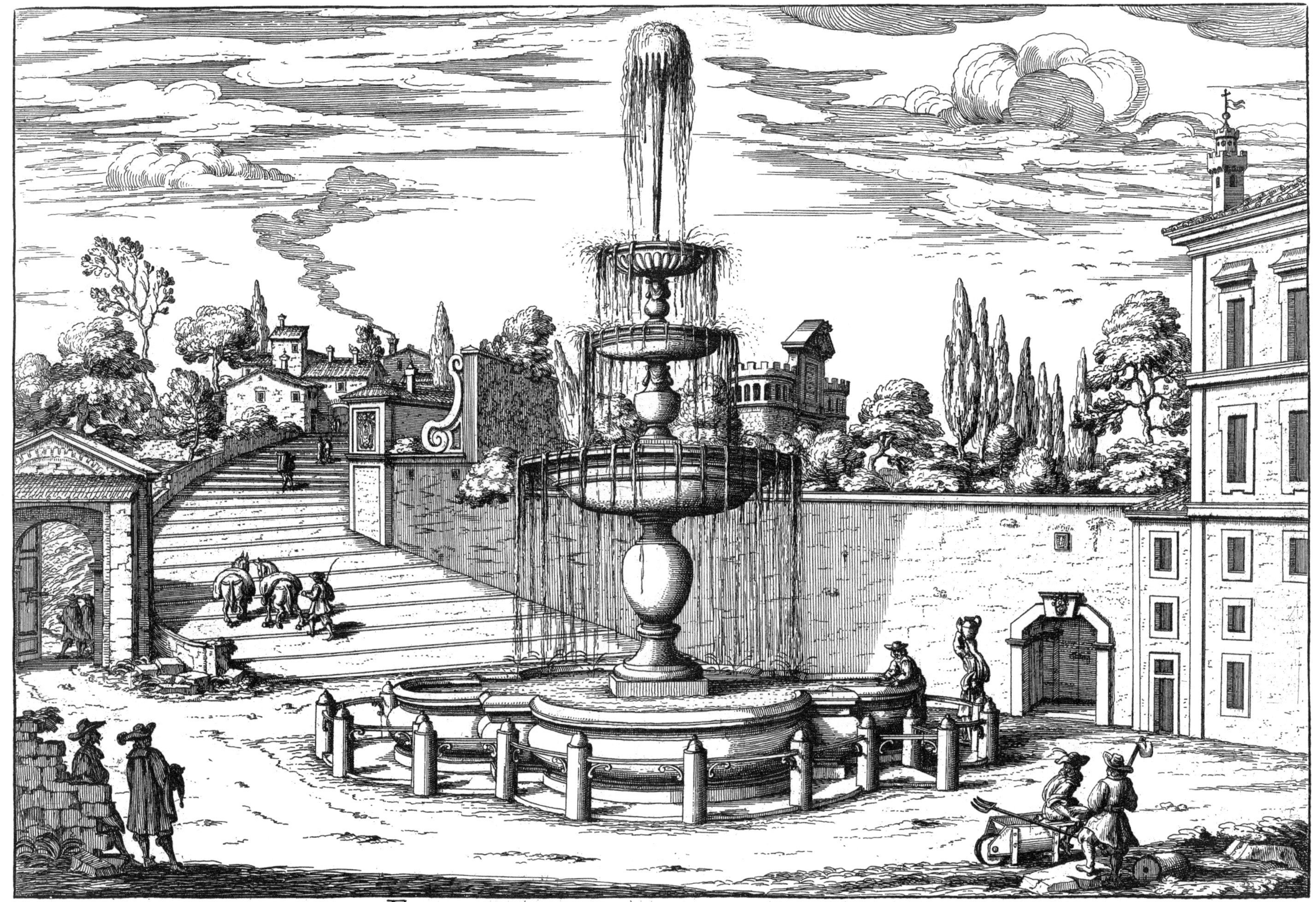

FONTANA NEL PALAZZO VATICANO

à piedi la scala, che va al forno, et auanti la porta, che entra in Beluedere, Archit.ᵃ di Carlo Maderno.

FOUNTAIN IN THE VATICAN PALACE, AT THE FOOT OF THE STAIRS LEADING TO THE BAKERY, AND IN FRONT OF THE DOOR TO BELVEDERE. ARCHITECTURE BY CARLO MADERNO.

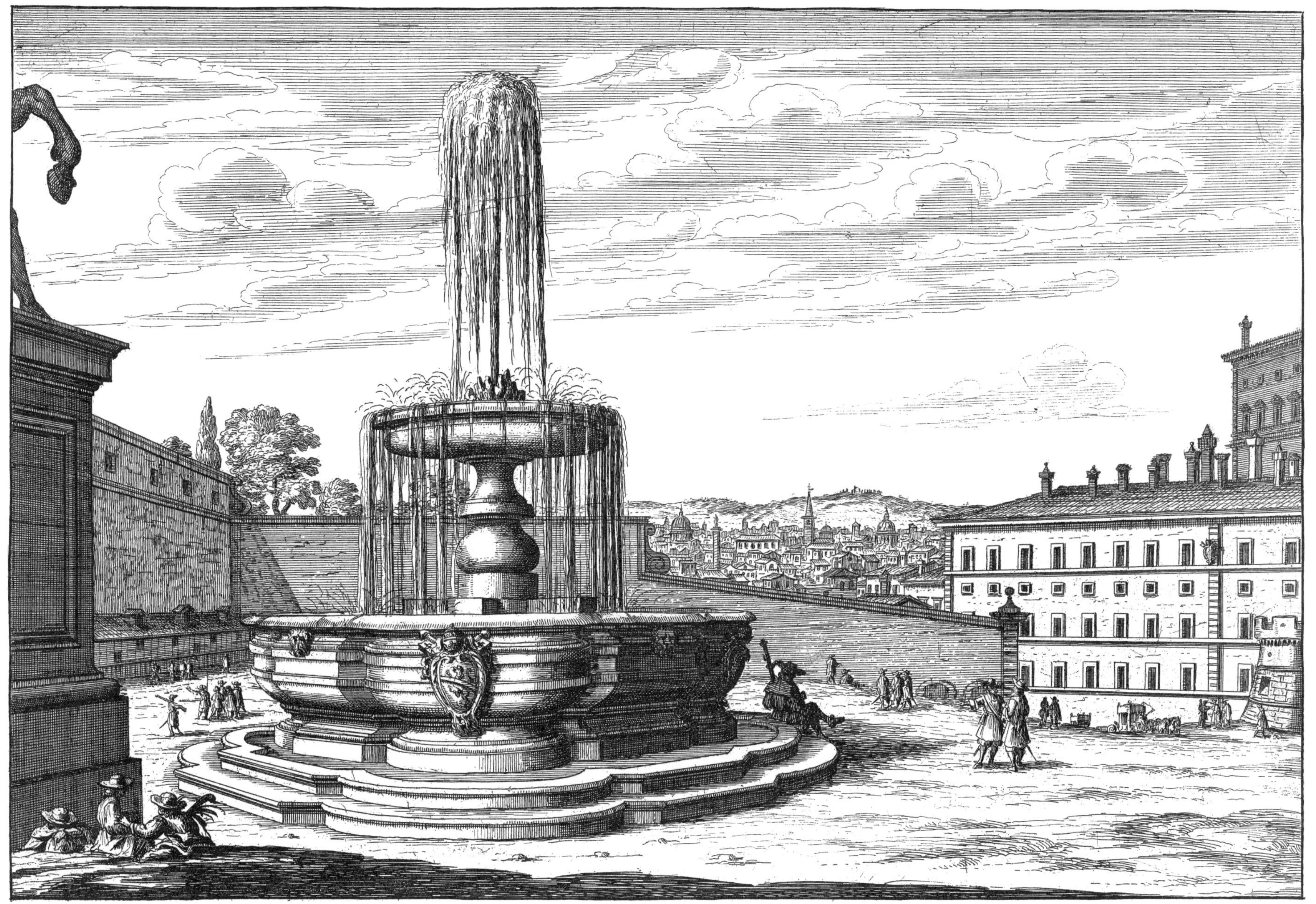

FONTANA SÙ LA PIAZZA DEL PALAZZO PONTIFICIO À MONTE CAVALLO.
Architettura del Cau.ͬ Domenico Fontana.

FOUNTAIN IN THE PIAZZA OF THE PAPAL PALACE IN MONTE CAVALLO. ARCHITECTURE BY SIR DOMENICO FONTANA.

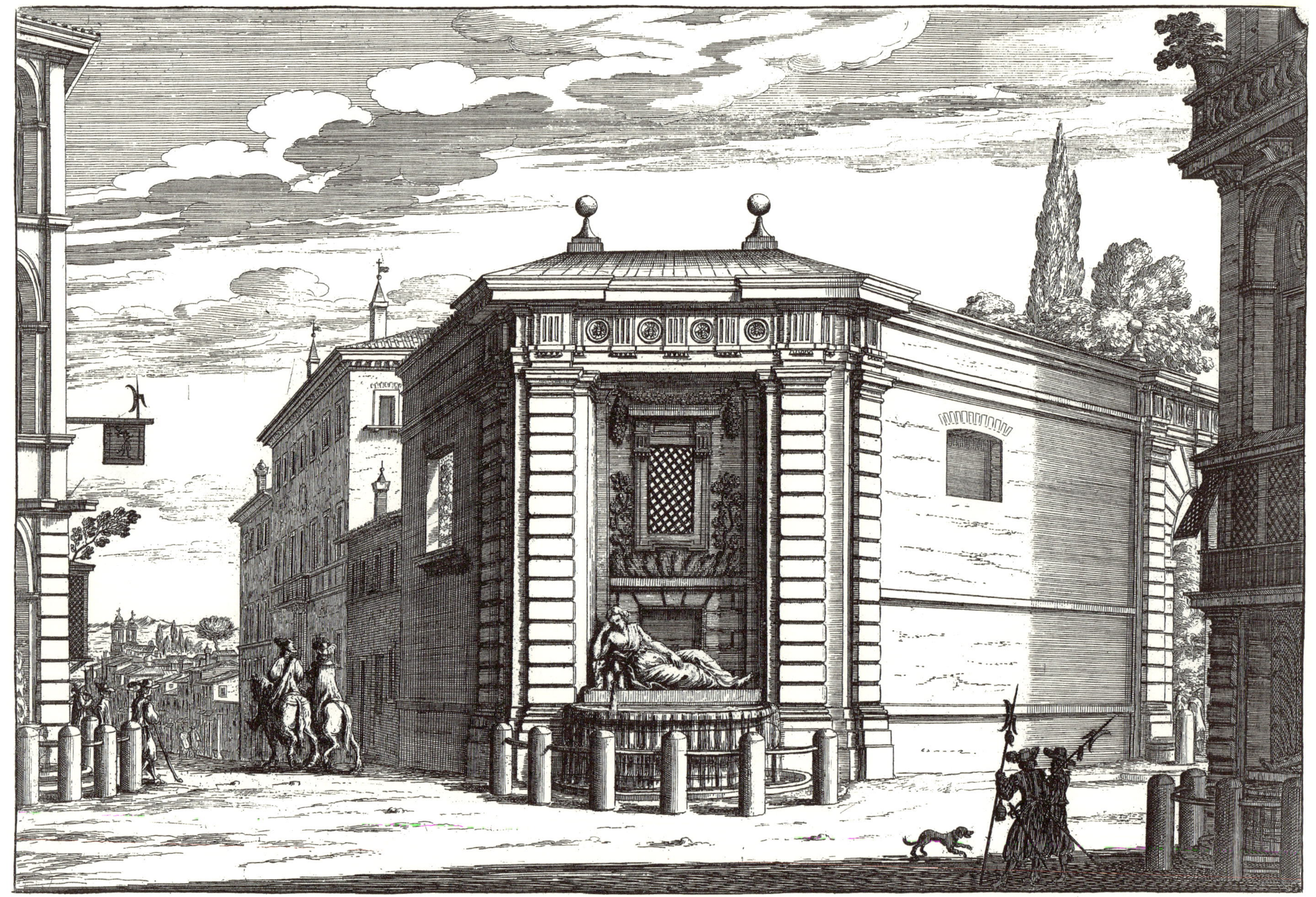

FONTANA DEL SIG. PRINCIPE DI PALLESTRINA
su'l canto del Giardino alle quattro Fontane, nel Rione de Monti Architet.ᵃ del Cau.Pietro Berrettini da Cortona.

FOUNTAIN OF THE PRINCE OF PALESTRINA, ON THE CORNER OF THE GARDEN OF THE FOUR FOUNTAINS IN THE MONTI DISTRICT.
ARCHITECTURE BY SIR PIETRO BERRETTINI OF CORTONA.

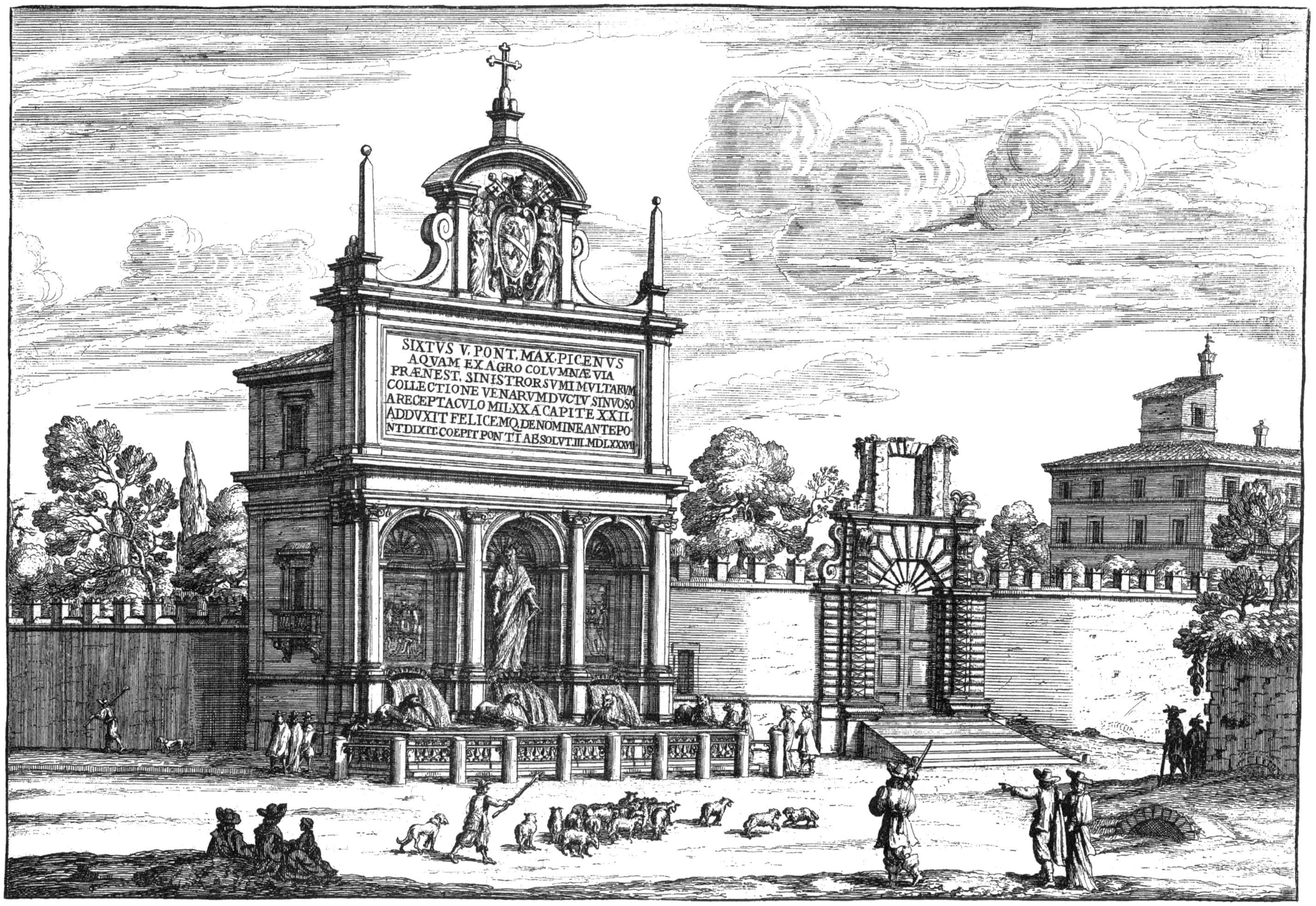

FONTANA E CASTELLO SVL MONTE VIMINALE
dell'Acqua della Colonna condotta da Sisto V. Architet.ª del Cau. Domenico Fontana

FOUNTAIN AND CASTLE ON THE VIMINAL HILL, WATER CHANNELED FROM THE COLONNA ESTATE BY POPE SIXTUS V.
ARCHITECTURE BY SIR DOMENICO FONTANA.

9

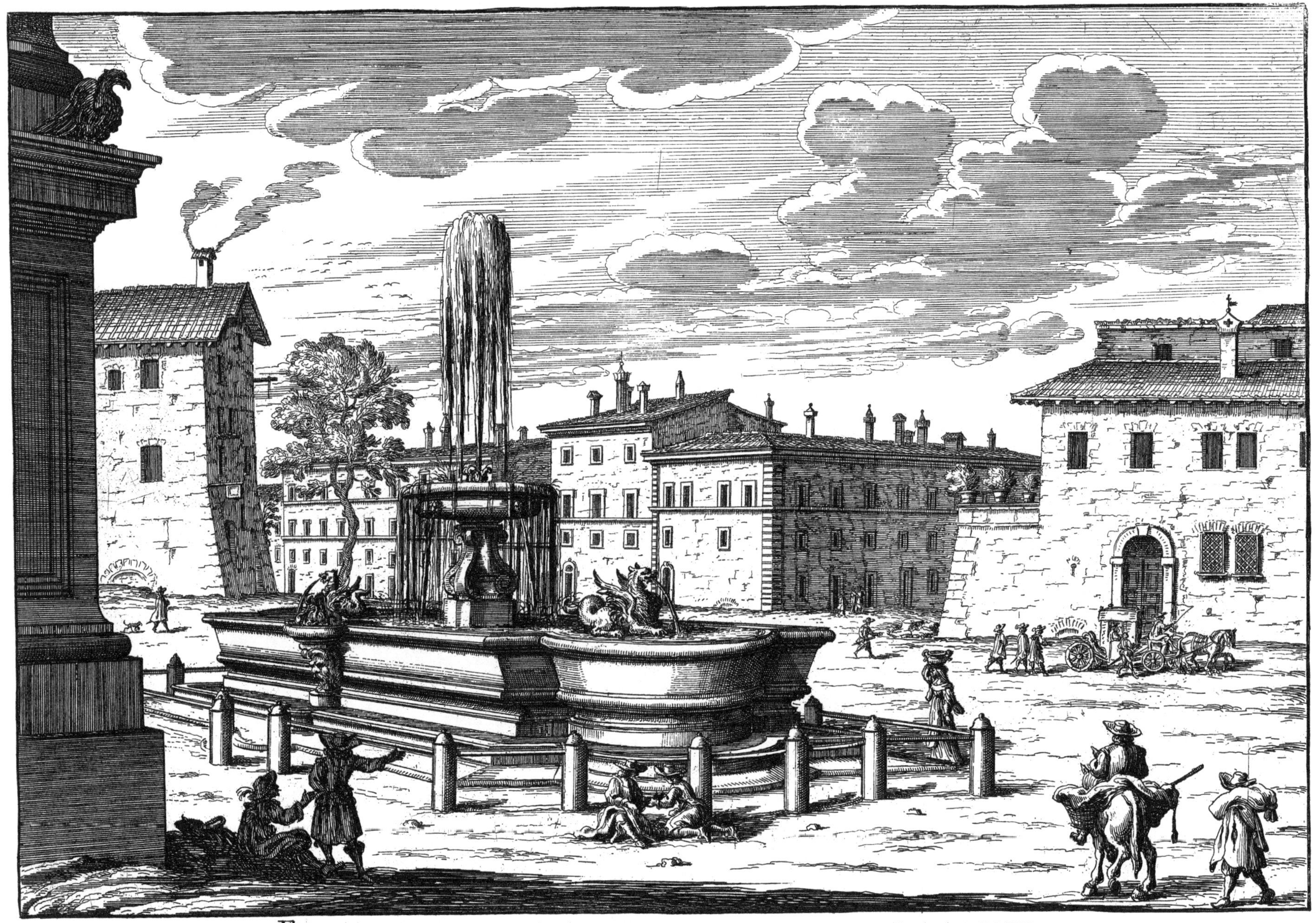

FONTANA NELLA PIAZZA DELLA BASILICA DI S. MARIA MAGGIORE
sotto la Colonna, verso il Laterano, Architet.ª del Cau. Carlo Maderno.

FOUNTAIN IN THE PIAZZA OF THE BASILICA OF SAINT MARY MAJOR, UNDER THE COLUMN, TOWARDS THE LATERAN.
ARCHITECTURE BY SIR CARLO MADERNO.

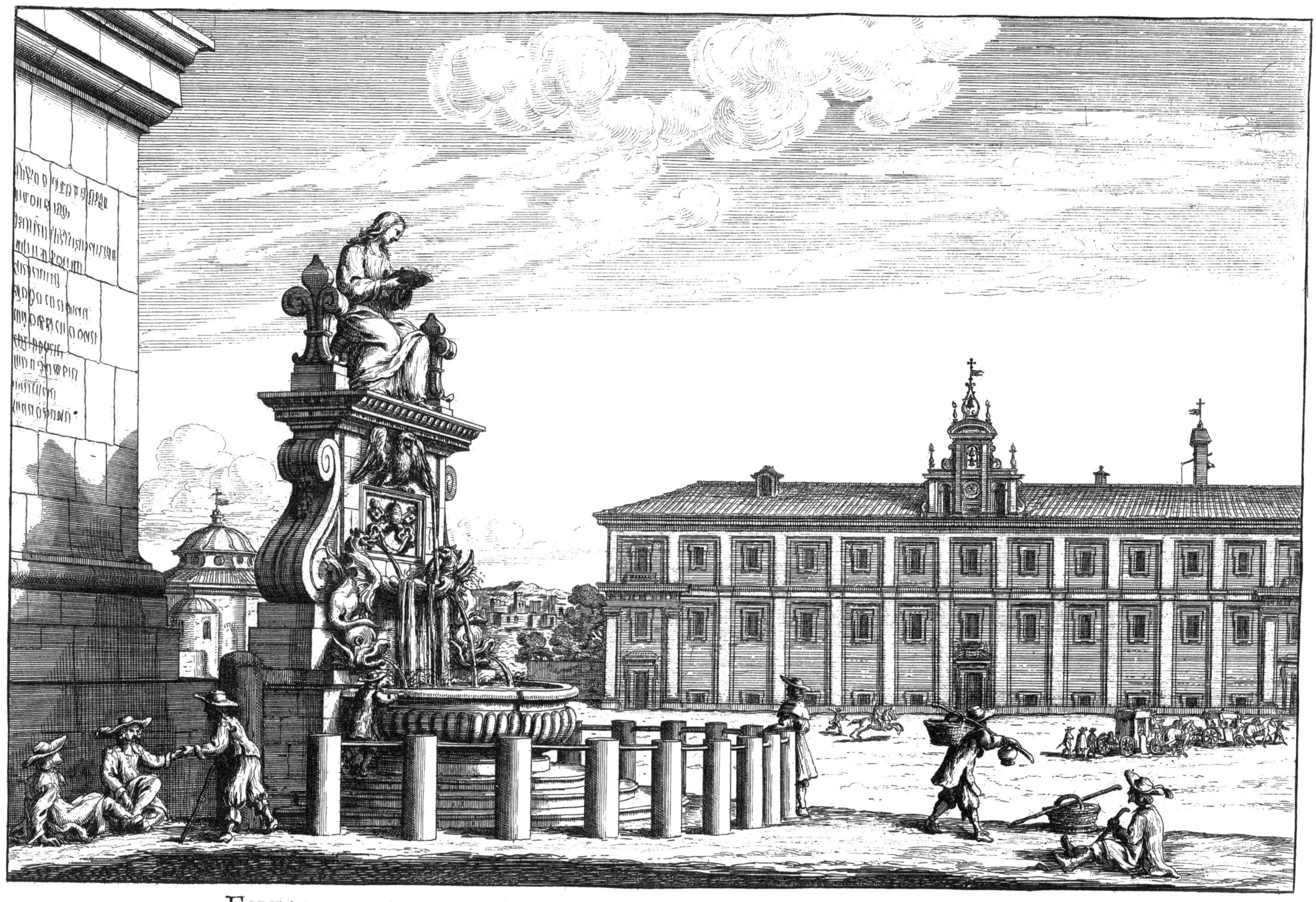

FONTANA NELLA PIAZZA DI S. GIOVANNI LATERANO SOTTO LA GVGLIA.

Architet.ª del Cau. Domenico Fontana.

FOUNTAIN IN THE PIAZZA OF ST. JOHN LATERAN UNDER THE OBELISK. ARCHITECTURE BY SIR DOMENICO FONTANA.

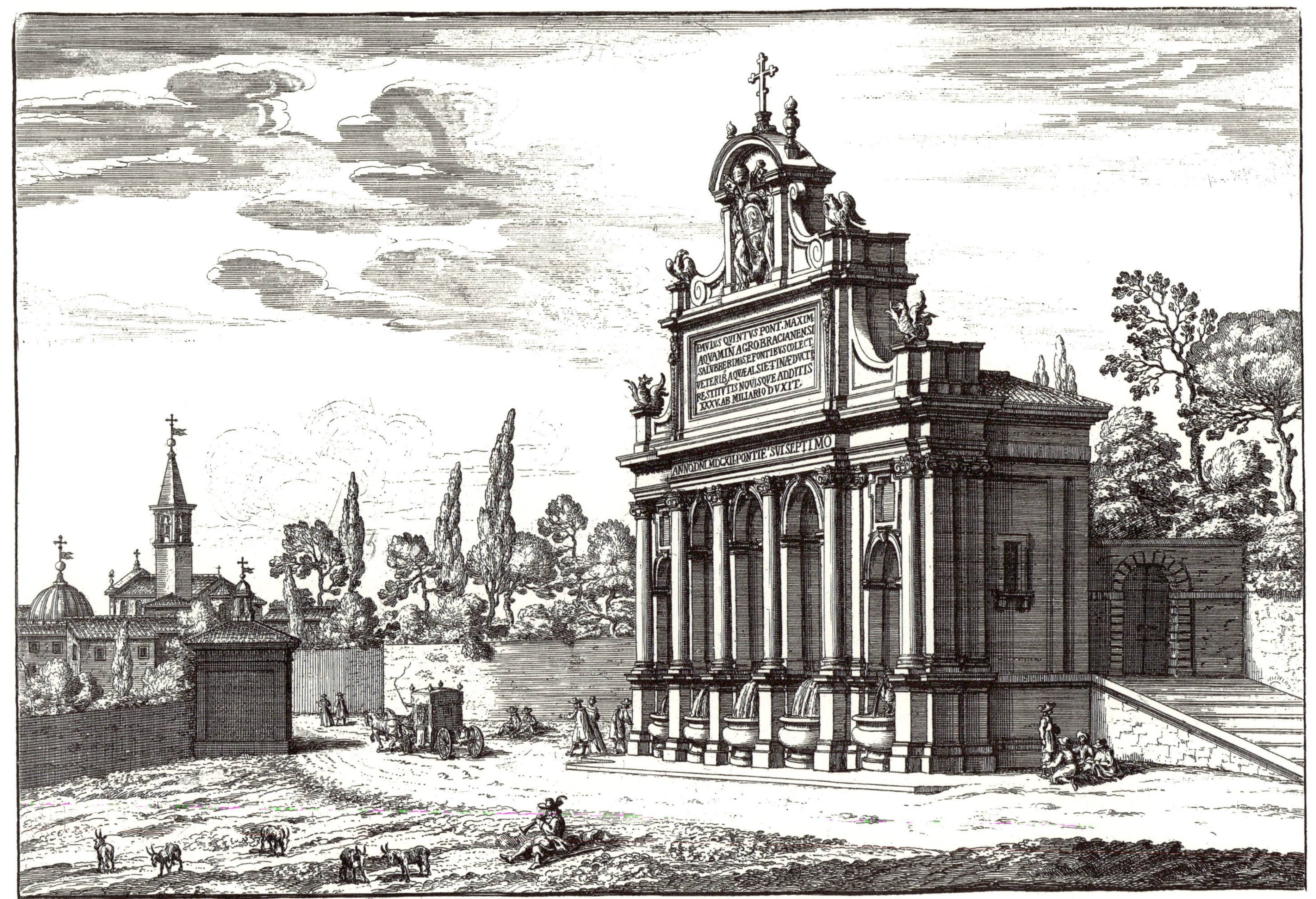

FONTANA, E CASTELLO DELL' ACQVA PAOLA

à S. Pietro Montorio, sù'l Gianicolo, condotta da Paolo V, uicino à Bracciano, Architet.ᵃ di Giouanni Fontana.

FOUNTAIN AND CASTLE OF THE ACQUA PAOLA IN SAN PIETRO IN MONTORIO ON THE JANICULUM HILL, CHANNELED FROM NEAR
LAKE BRACCIANO BY POPE PAUL V. ARCHITECTURE BY GIOVANNI FONTANA.

12

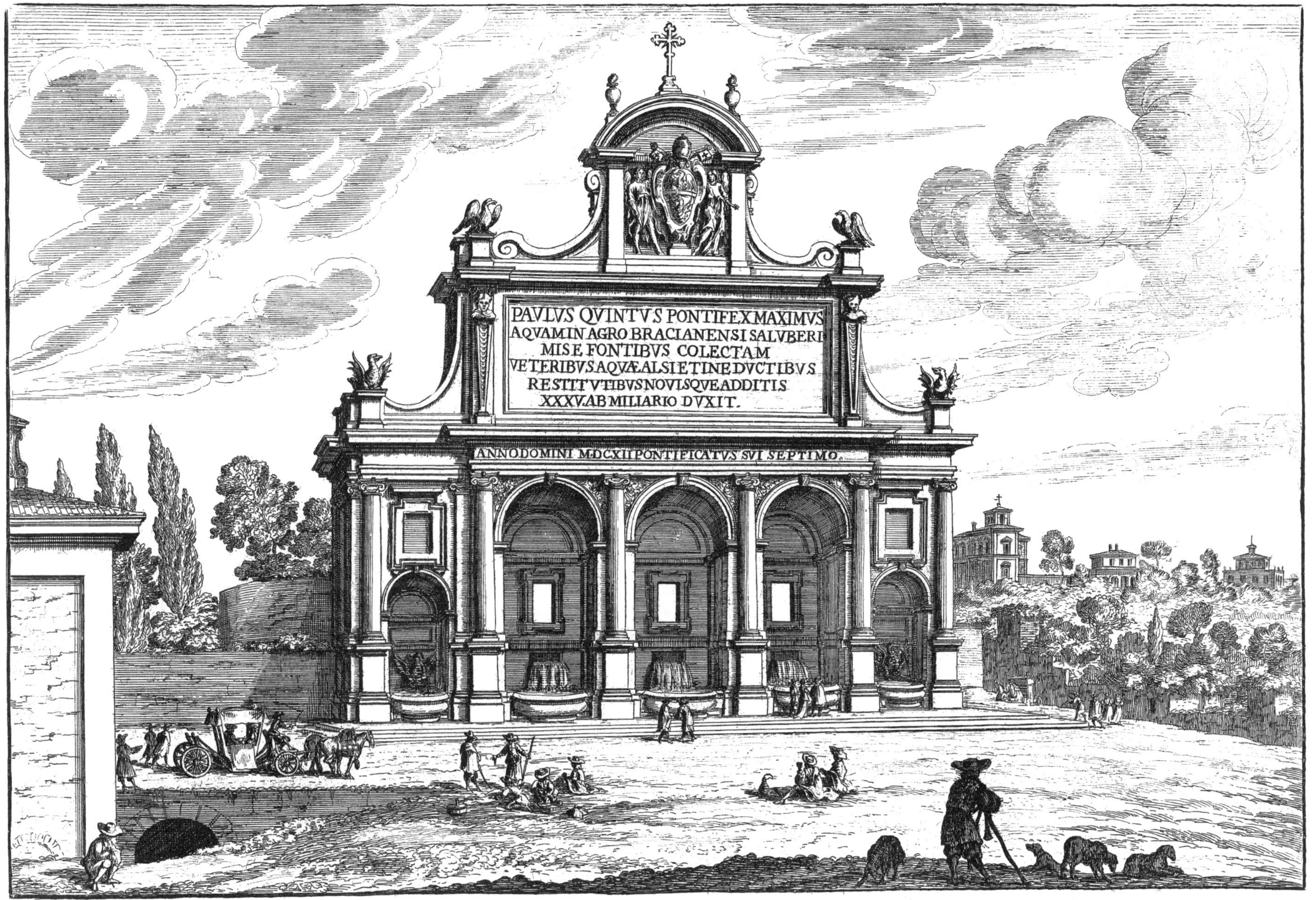

ALTRA VEDVTA DELLA FONTANA, E CASTELLO DELL' ACQVA PAOLA.
à S.Pietro Montorio, su'l Gianicolo condotta da Paolo V. vicino à Bracciano Architet.o di Giouanni Fontana.

ALTERNATE VIEW OF THE FOUNTAIN AND CASTLE OF THE ACQUA PAOLA IN SAN PIETRO IN MONTORIO ON THE JANICULUM HILL,
CHANNELED FROM NEAR LAKE BRACCIANO BY POPE PAUL V. ARCHITECTURE BY GIOVANNI FONTANA.

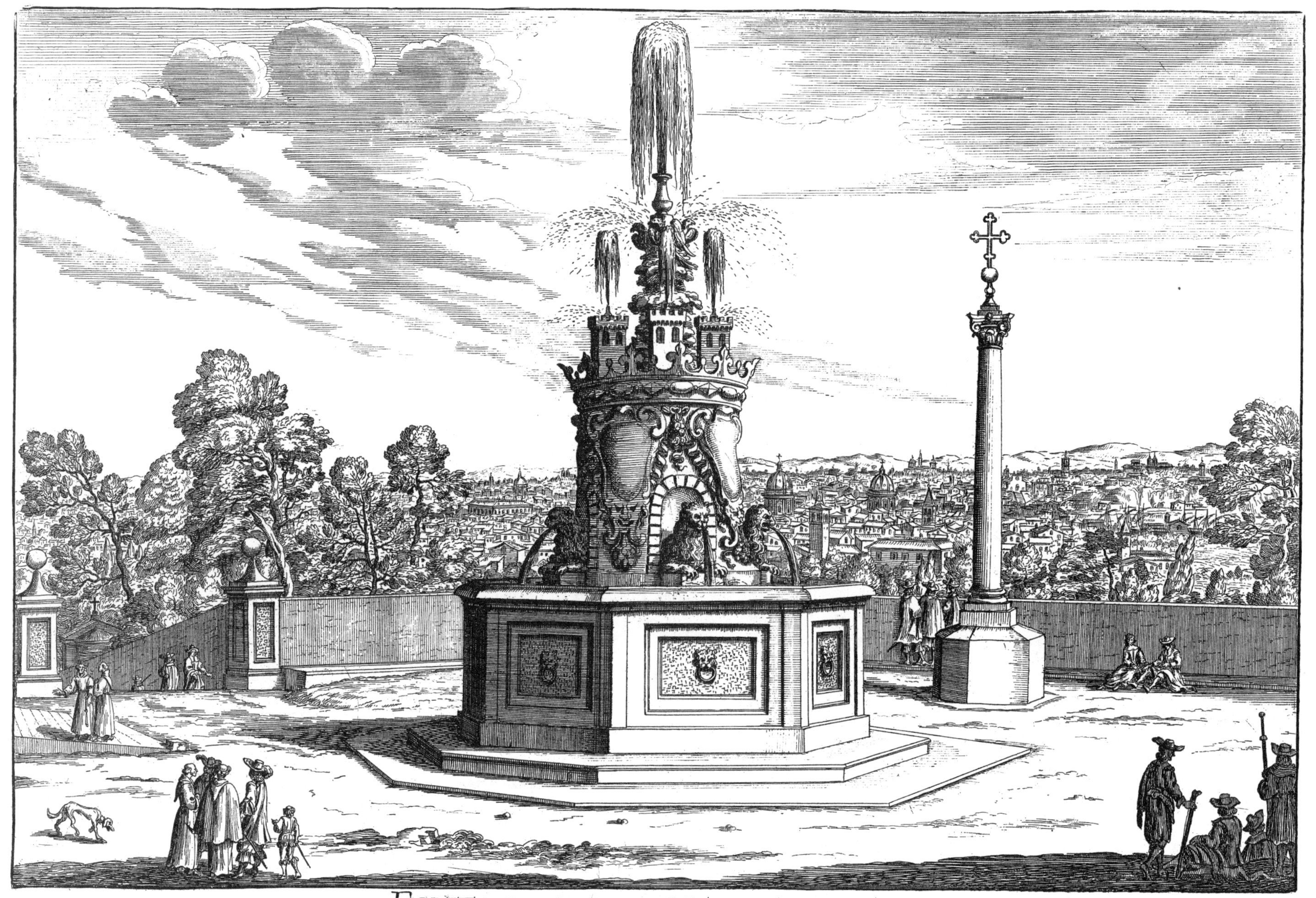

FOUNTAIN ON THE JANICULUM HILL, IN FRONT OF THE CHURCH OF SAN PIETRO IN MONTORIO. ARCHITECTURE BY GIOVANNI FONTANA.

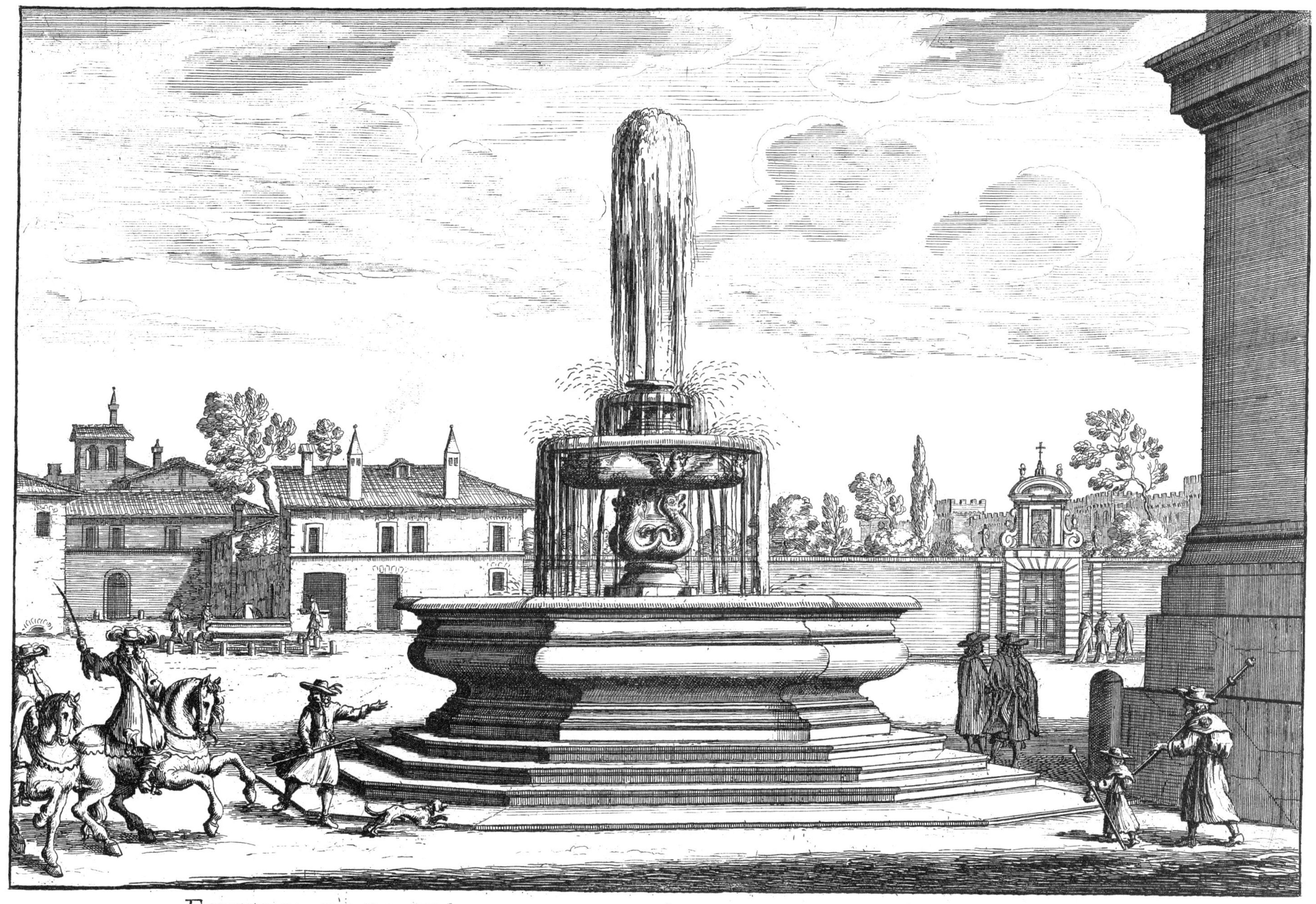

FONTANA SV LA PIAZZA DELLA PORTA DEL POPOLO SOTTO LA GVGLIA.

Architet.ᵃ del Cau. Domenico Fontana.

FOUNTAIN IN THE PIAZZA OF PORTA DEL POPOLO UNDER THE OBELISK. ARCHITECTURE BY SIR DOMENICO FONTANA.

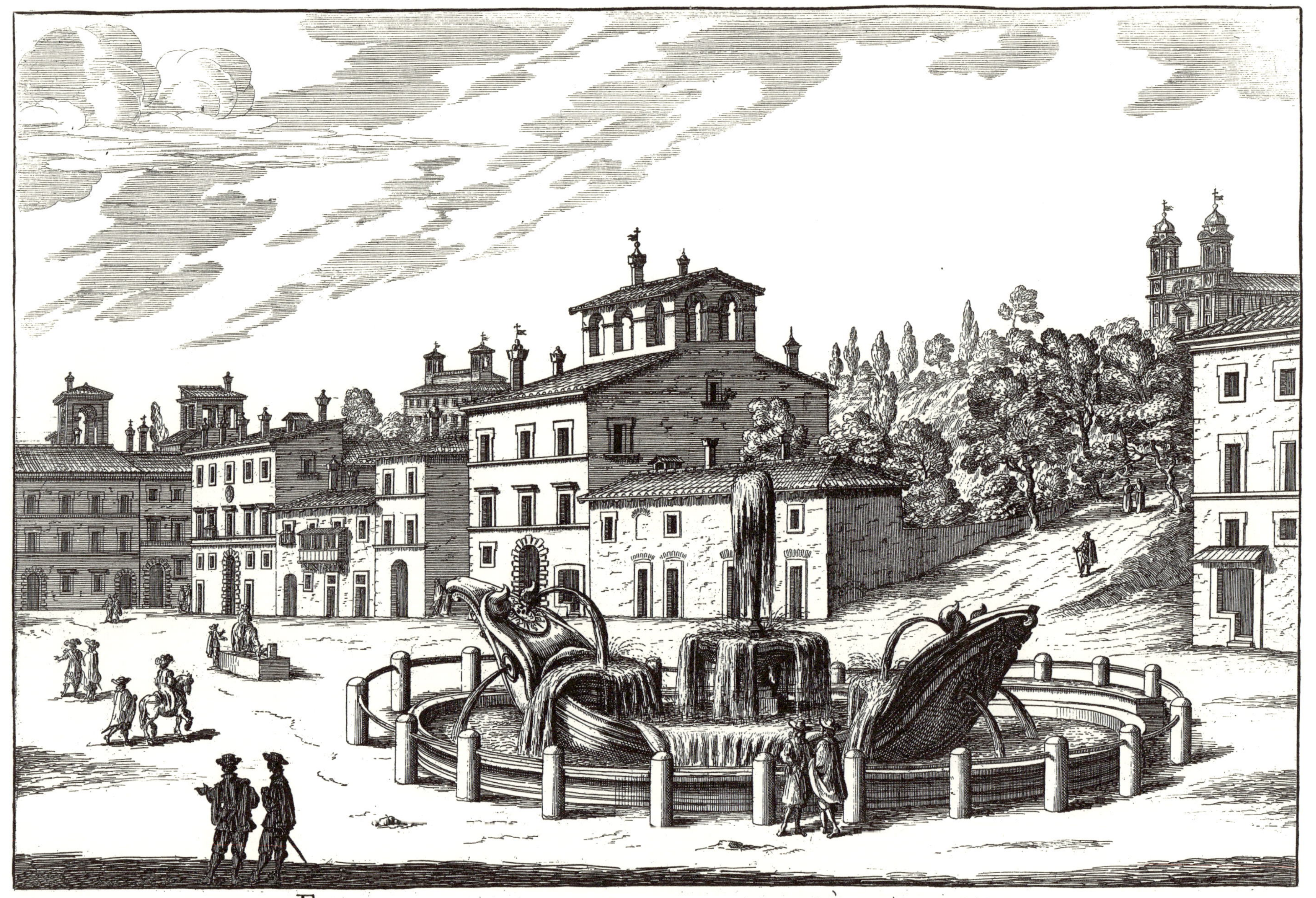

FONTANA NELLA PIAZZA DELLA TRINITÀ DE MONTI,
nel Rione di Campo Marzo, Architet.ª del Cau. Gio. Lorenzo Bernini.

FOUNTAIN IN PIAZZA TRINITÀ DEI MONTI, IN THE CAMPO MARZIO DISTRICT. ARCHITECTURE BY SIR GIO. LORENZO BERNINI.

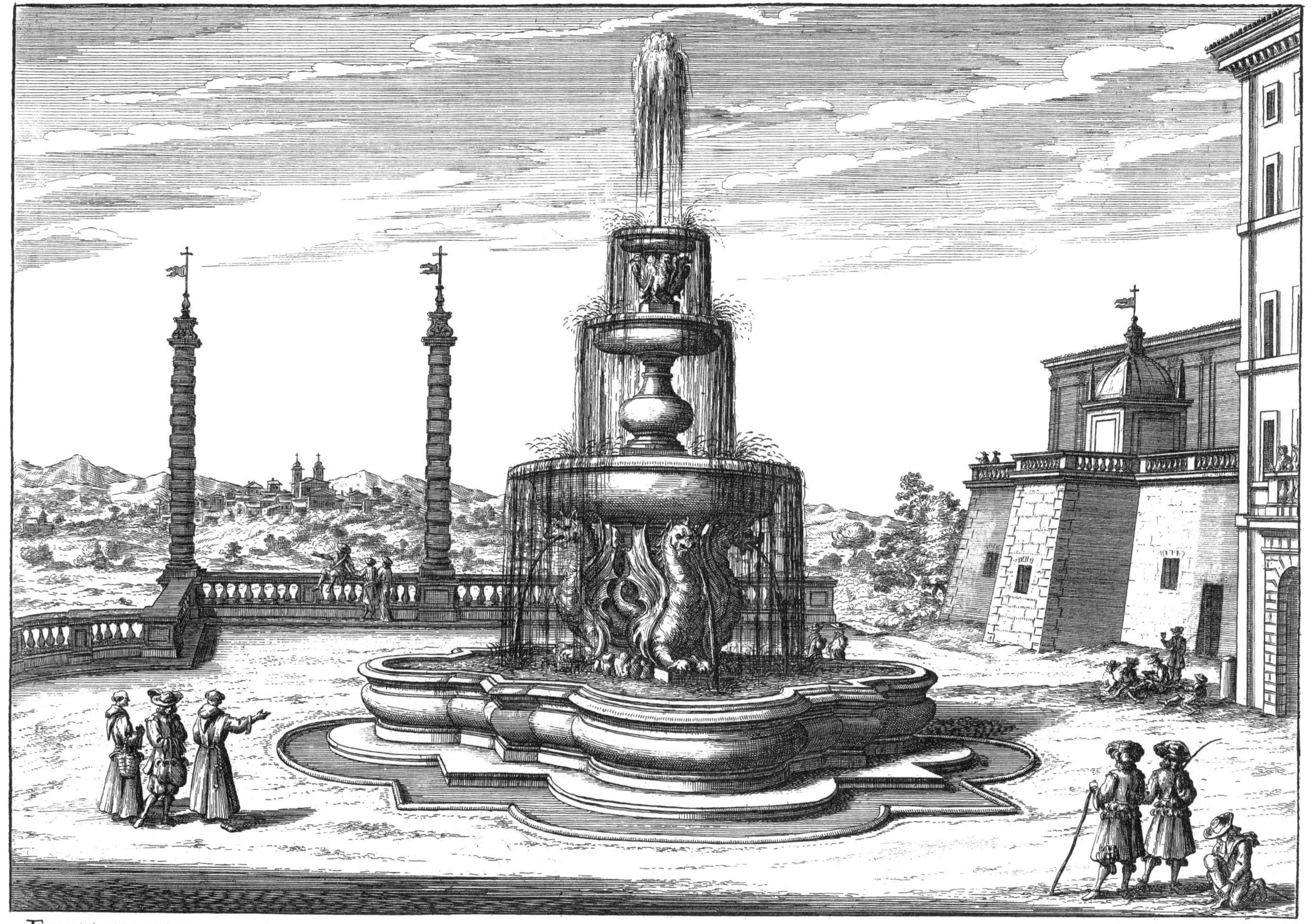

FONTANA NELLA VILLA BORGHESE DI MONDRAGONE A FRASCATI, CHE VERSA AVANTI IL PALAZZO ARCHITETTV-RA DI GIOVANNI FONTANA.

FOUNTAIN STANDING IN FRONT OF VILLA MONDRAGONE BORGHESE IN FRASCATI. ARCHITECTURE BY GIOVANNI FONTANA.

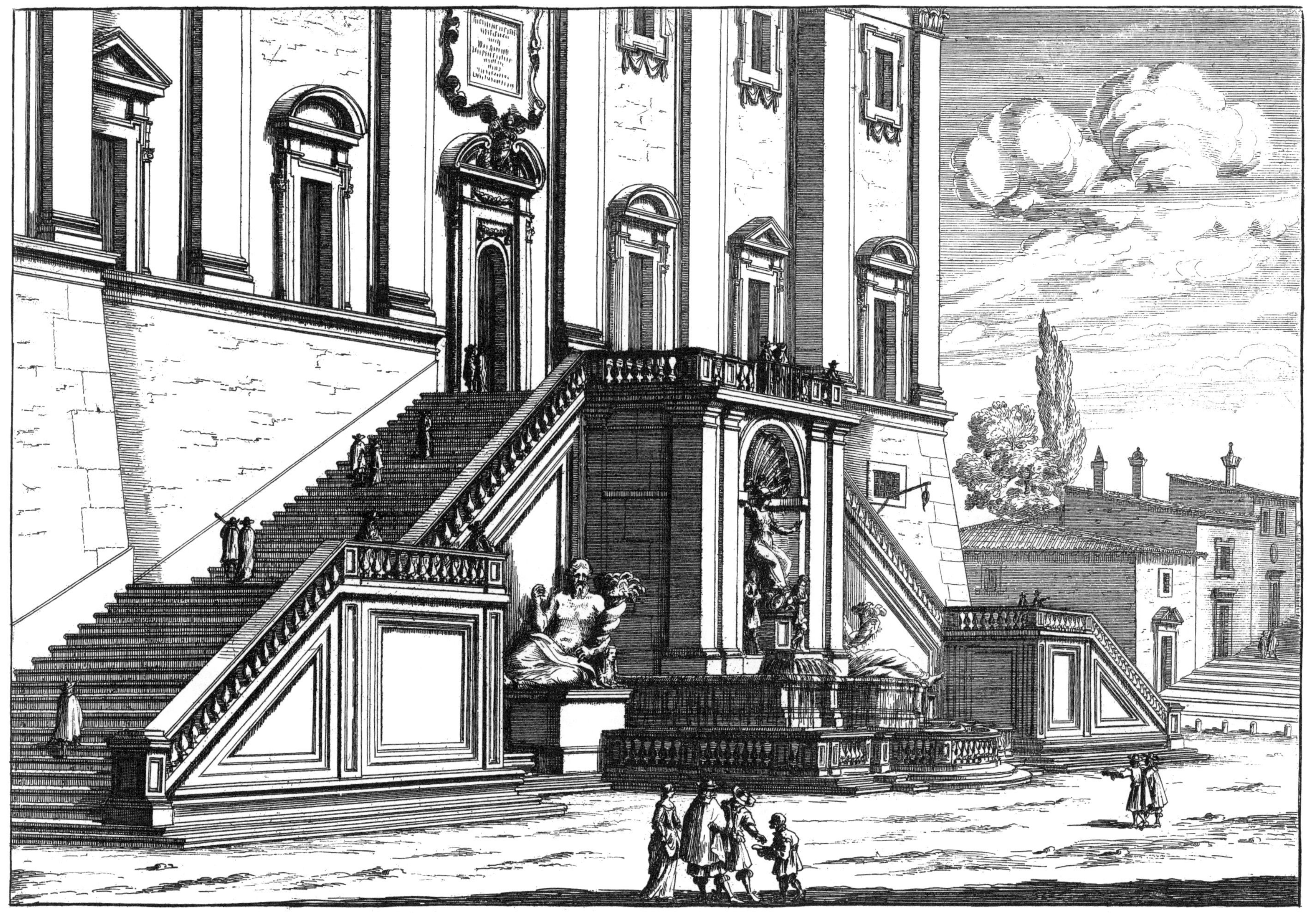

FONTANA SV LA PIAZZA DEL CAMPIDOGLIO
che fà ornamento alle scale del Palazzo del Senatore di Roma, Architettura di Michel'Angelo Buonaroti.

FOUNTAIN IN PIAZZA OF CAPITOLINE HILL ADORNING THE STAIRS OF THE SENATORIAL PALACE.
ARCHITECTURE BY MICHELANGELO BUONARROTI.

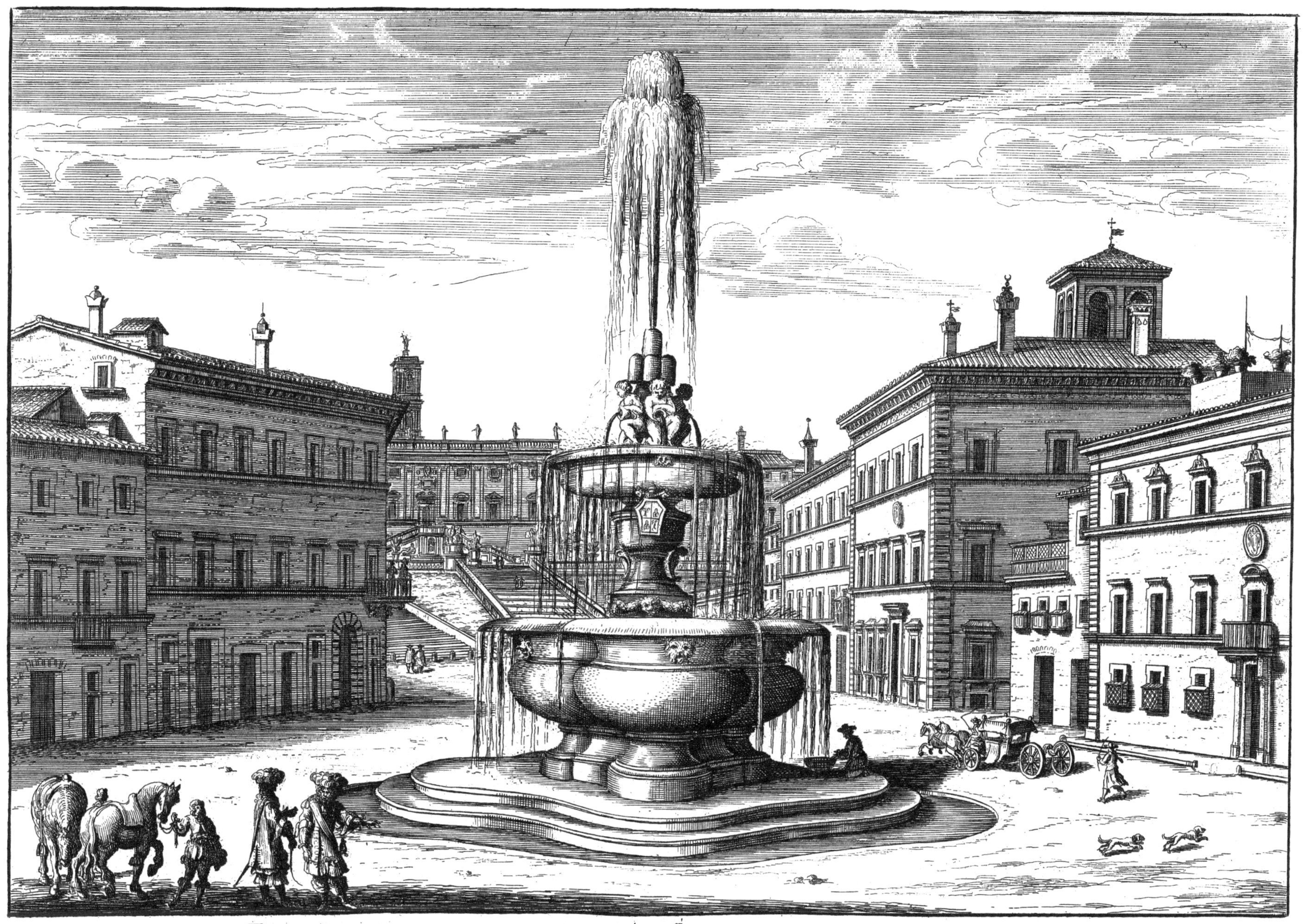

FOUNTAIN IN THE PIAZZA OF THE MUTI FAMILY UNDER THE CAPITOLINE HILL. ARCHITECTURE BY GIACOMO DELLA PORTA.

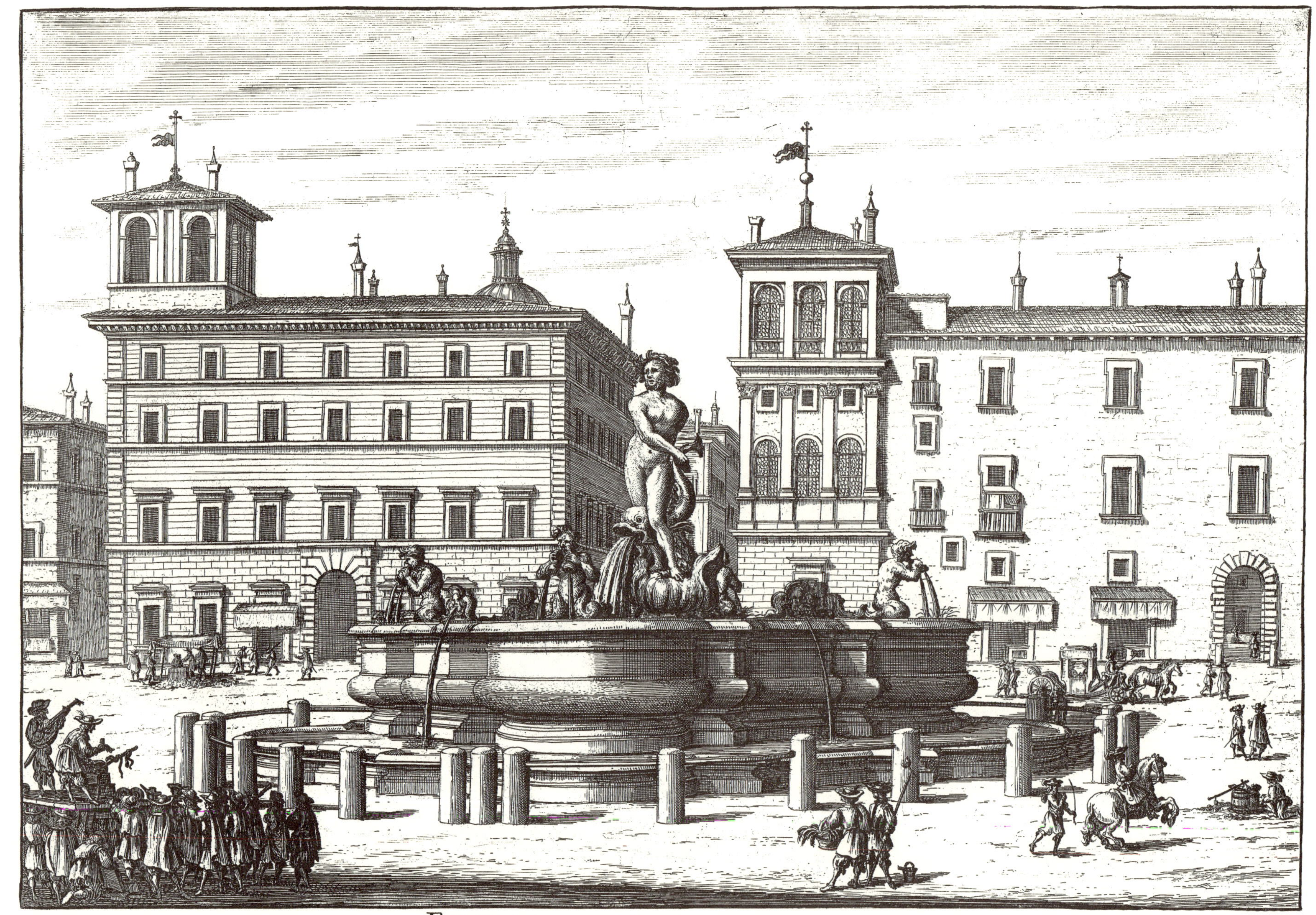

FONTANA IN PIAZZA NAVONA.

auanti il Palazzo del Ecc.ᵐᵃ Sig. Principe Pamphilio, Architettura di Giacomo della Porta, riſtaurata dal Cauᵛ·Bernini,et abbellita cõ la statua di Nettuno·

FOUNTAIN IN PIAZZA NAVONA IN FRONT OF THE PALACE OF HIS EXCELLENCY THE PRINCE PAMPHILI. ARCHITECTURE BY GIACOMO DELLA PORTA, RESTORED BY SIR BERNINI, AND ADORNED WITH THE STATUE OF NEPTUNE.

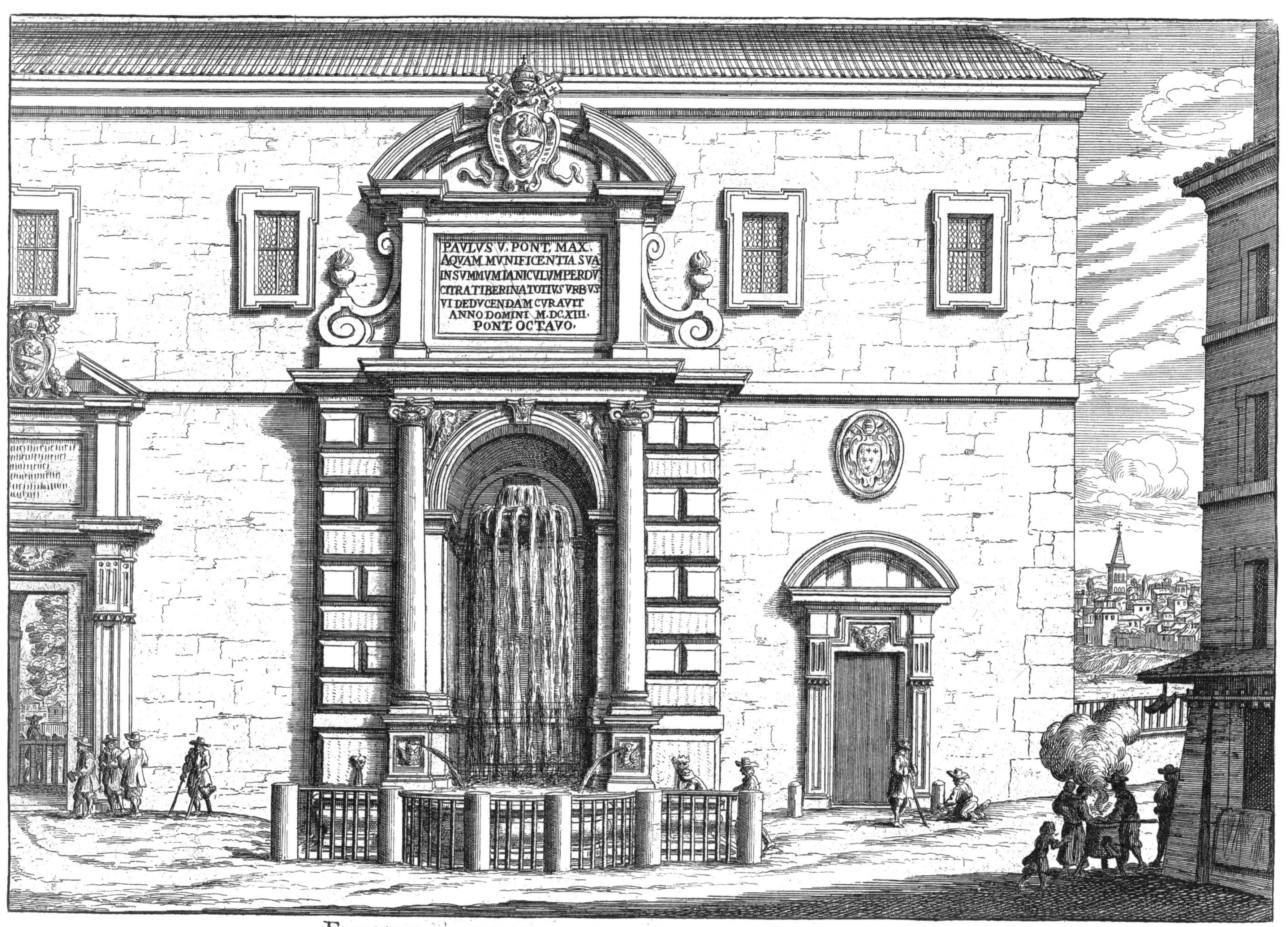

FONTANA A PONTE SISTO IN CAPO STRADA GIVLIA,
nel Rione della Regola Architettura del Cau Domenico Fontana

FOUNTAIN AT PONTE SISTO AT THE ENTRANCE TO VIA GIULIA, IN THE REGOLA DISTRICT. ARCHITECTURE BY SIR DOMENICO FONTANA.

21

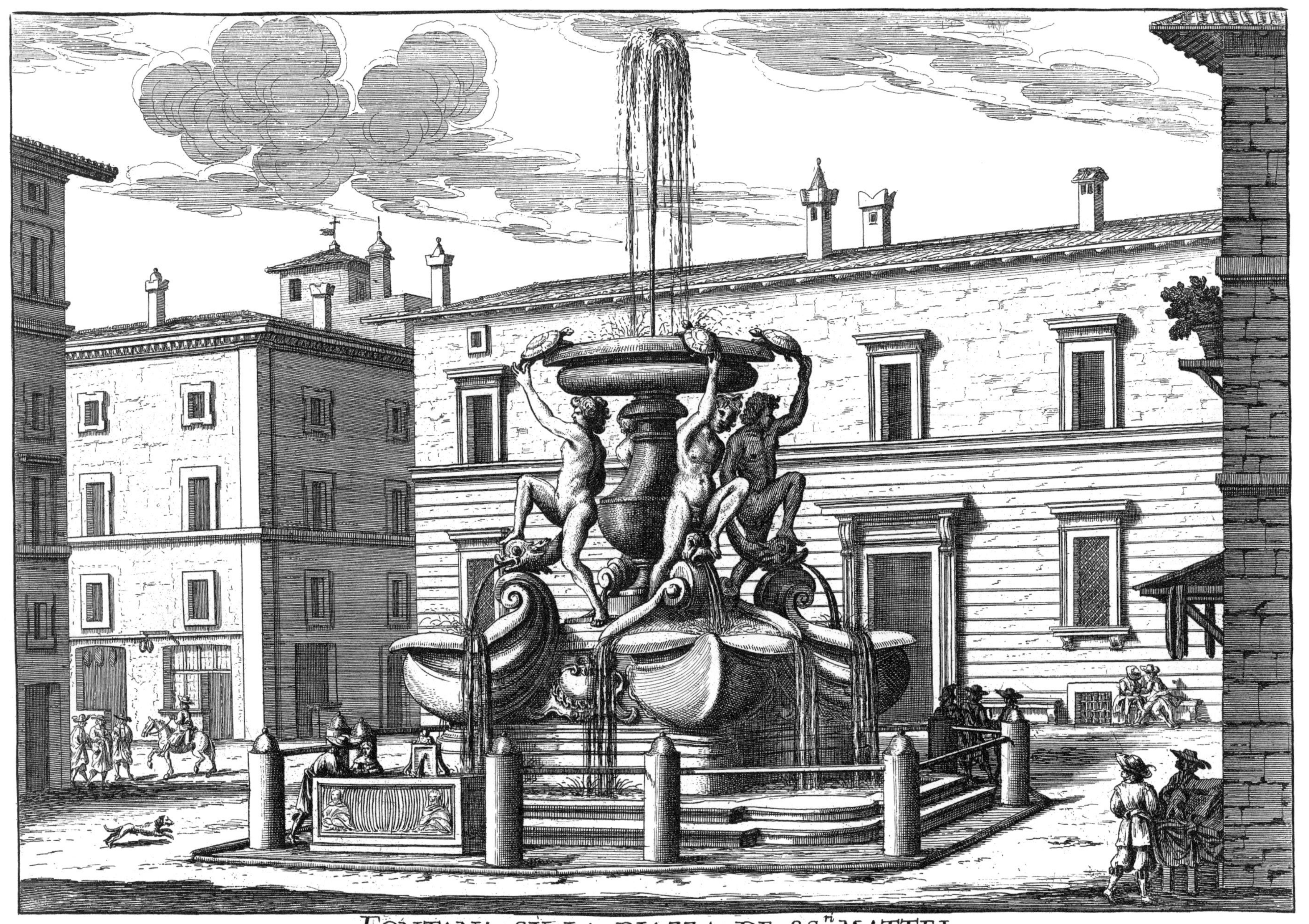

FOUNTAIN IN PIAZZA MATTEI IN THE S. ANGELO DISTRICT. ARCHITECTURE BY GIACOMO DELLA PORTA.

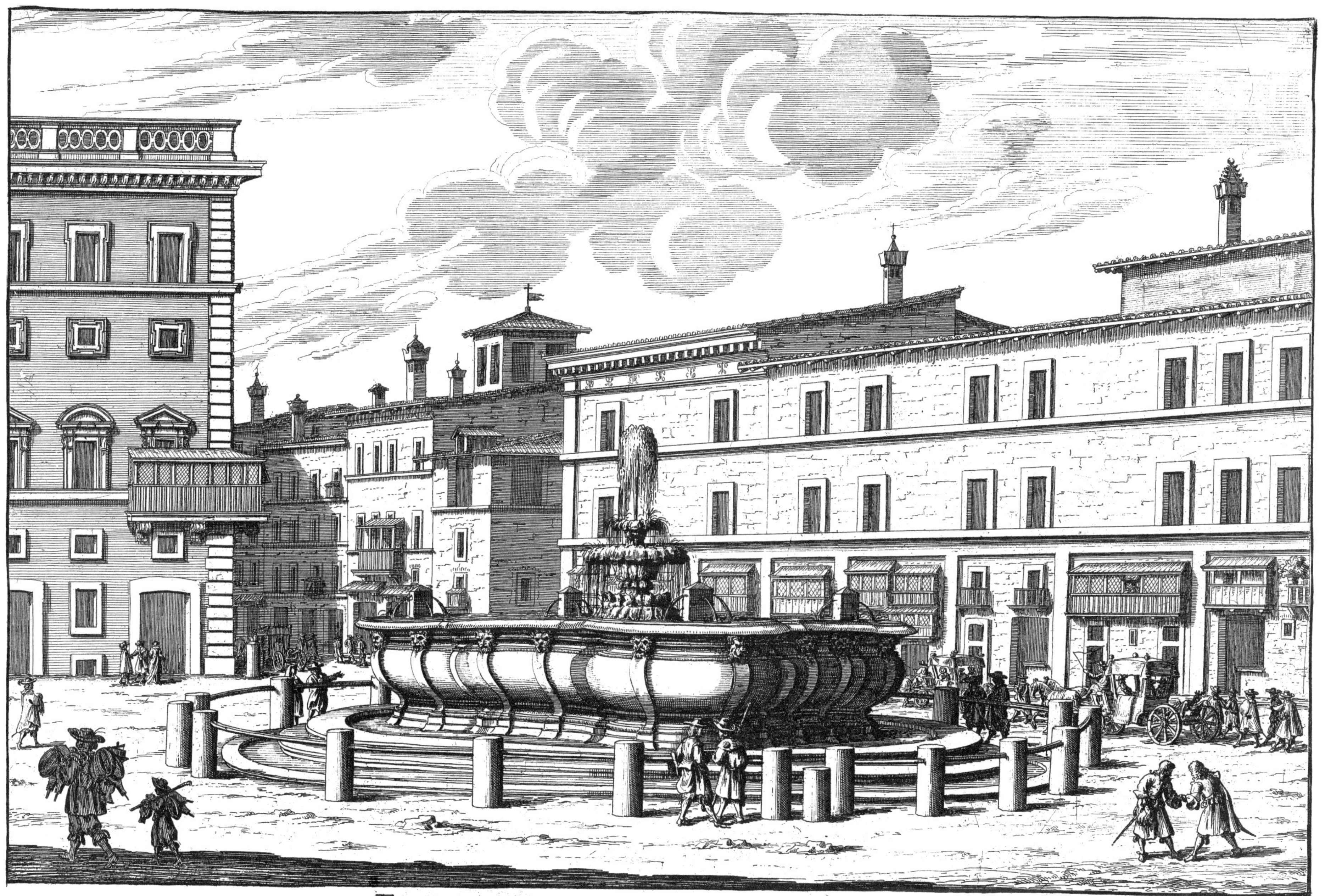

FONTANA IN PIAZZA COLONNA
Architet.ª di Giacomo della Porta.

FOUNTAIN IN PIAZZA COLONNA. ARCHITECTURE BY GIACOMO DELLA PORTA.

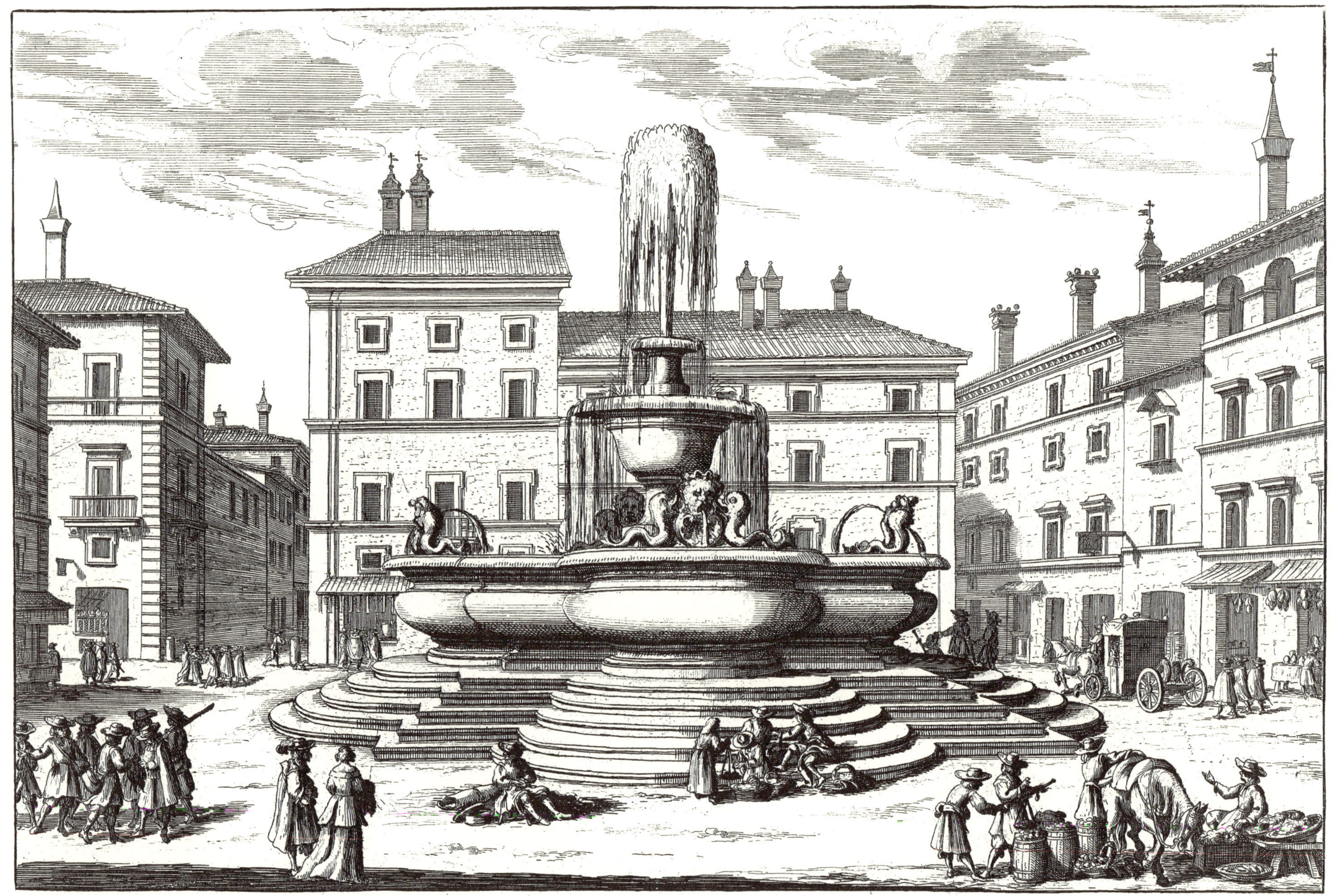

Fontana nella Piazza della Rotonda.

e Rione di Colonna, Architet.ᵃ di Giacomo della Porta.

FOUNTAIN IN PIAZZA DELLA ROTONDA, AND COLONNA DISTRICT. ARCHITECTURE BY GIACOMO DELLA PORTA.

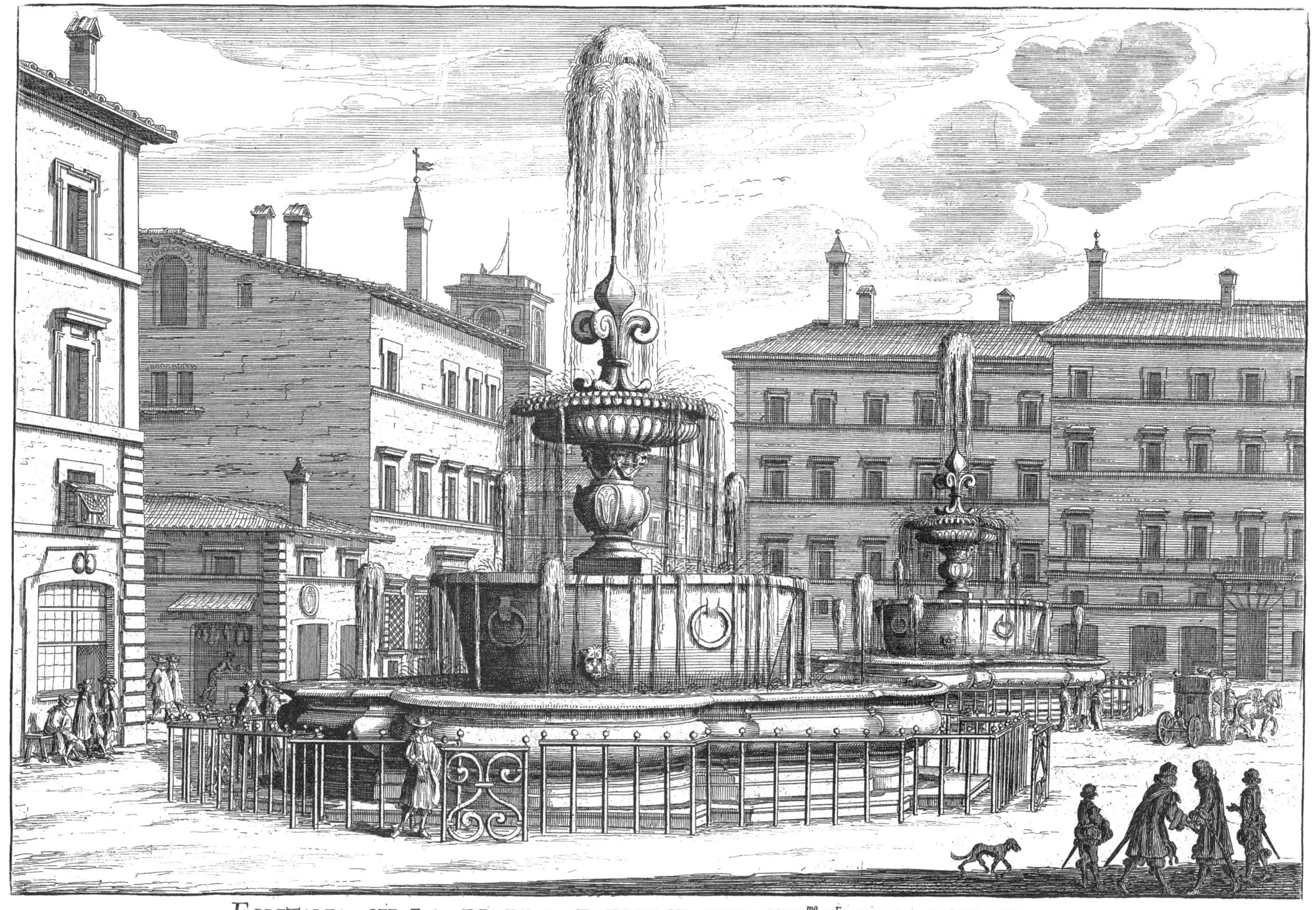

FOUNTAIN OF HIS HIGHNESS THE DUKE OF PARMA IN PIAZZA FARNESE, IN THE REGOLA DISTRICT. ARCHITECTURE BY SIR GIROLAMO RAINALDI.

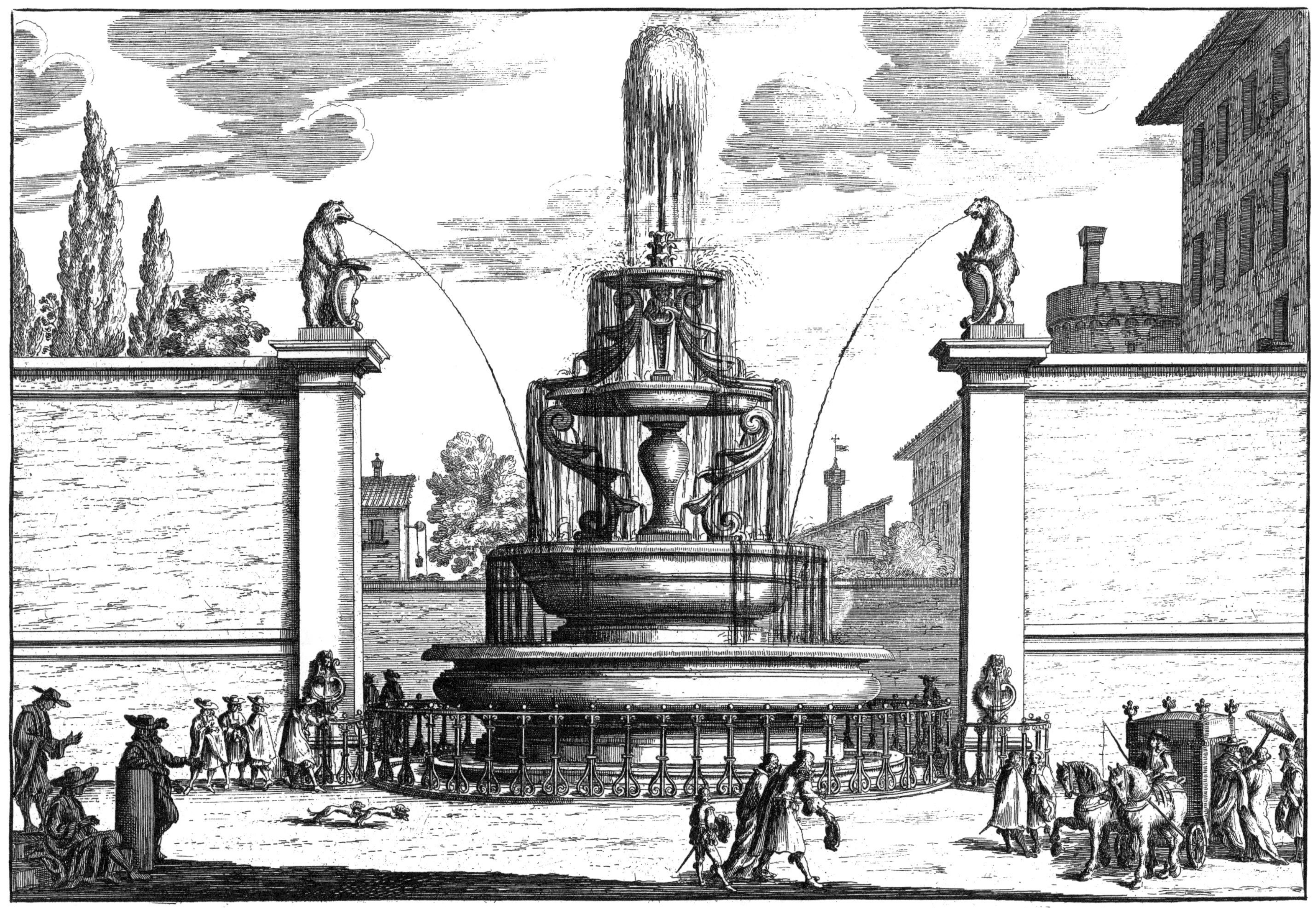

FONTANA NEL CORTILE DEL PALAZZO DEL SIG. DVCA DI BRACCIANO,
à Monte Giordano, nel Rione di Ponte, Architet.ª di Antonio Casoni.

FOUNTAIN IN THE COURTYARD OF THE PALACE OF THE DUKE OF BRACCIANO, IN MONTE GIORDANO, PONTE DISTRICT.
ARCHITECTURE BY ANTONIO CASONI.

26

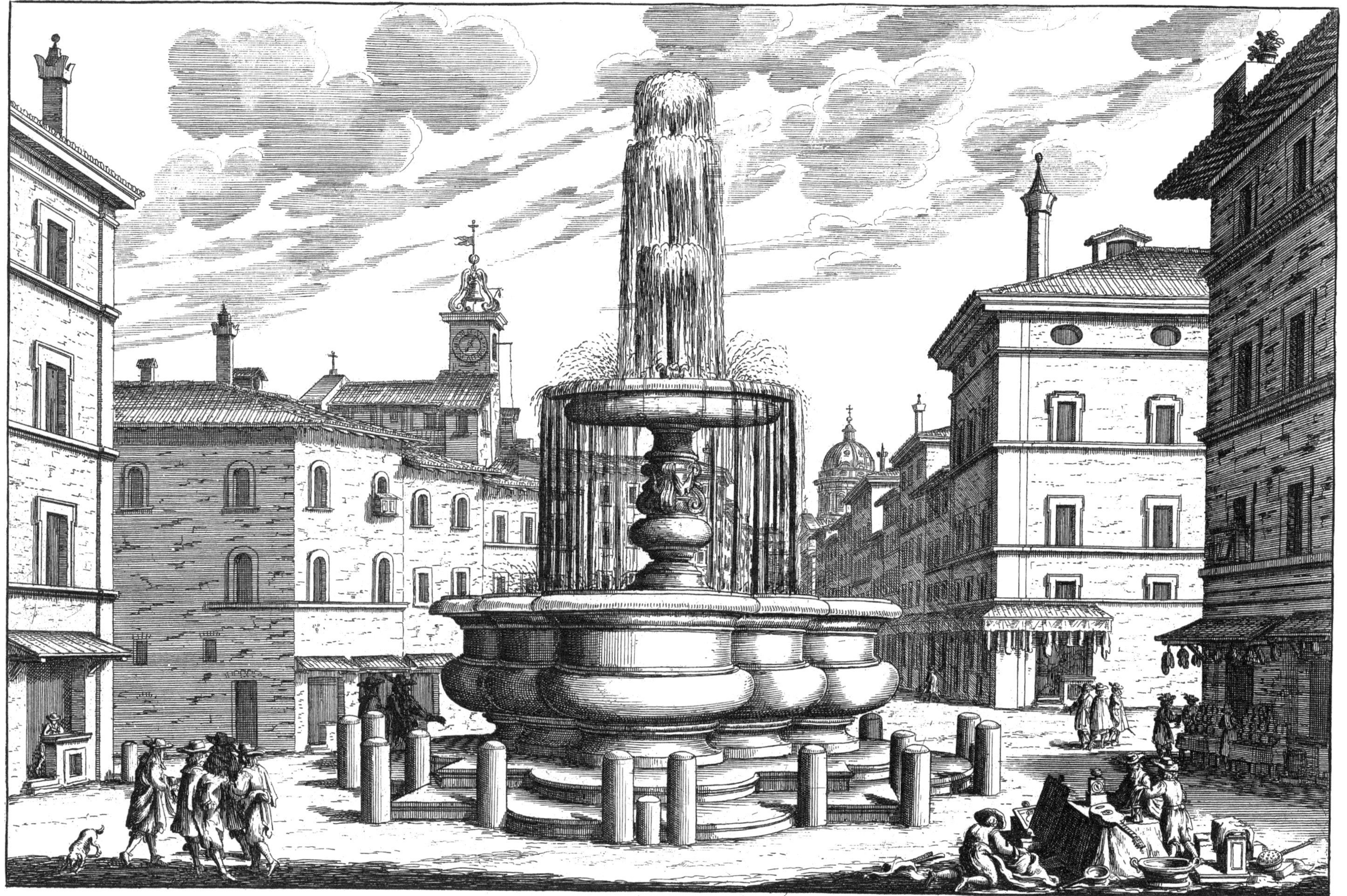

FOUNTAIN IN PIAZZA GIUDEA, IN THE REGOLA DISTRICT. ARCHITECTURE BY GIACOMO DELLA PORTA.

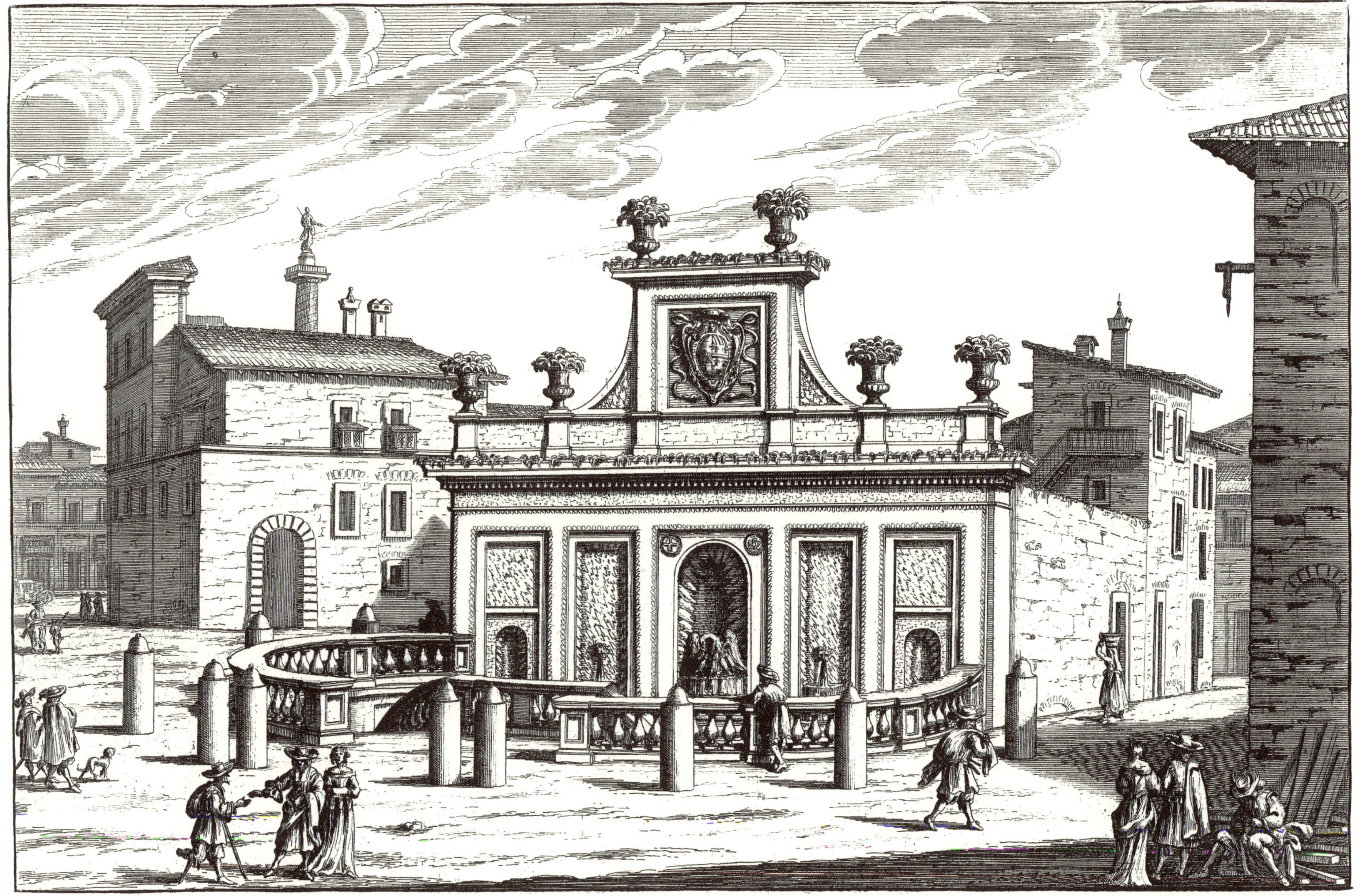

FONTANA A MONTE CITORIO

Rione di Colonna, Architettura di Francesco da Volterra.

FOUNTAIN IN MONTE CITORIO, IN THE COLONNA DISTRICT. ARCHITECTURE BY FRANCESCO DA VOLTERRA.

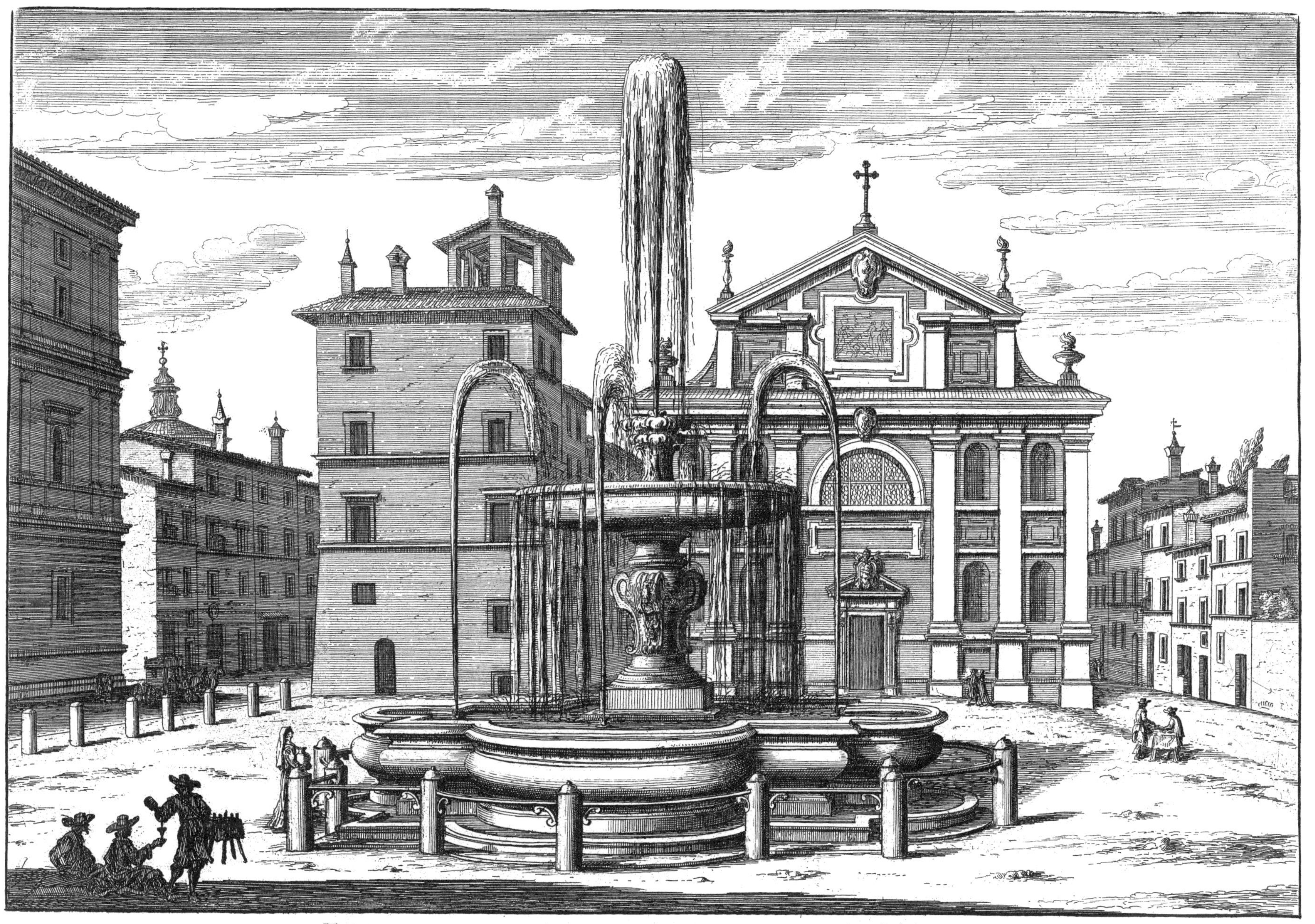

FOUNTAIN IN THE PIAZZA OF S. GIACOMO A SCOSSACAVALLI, IN THE BORGO DISTRICT. ARCHITECTURE BY SIR CARLO MADERNO.

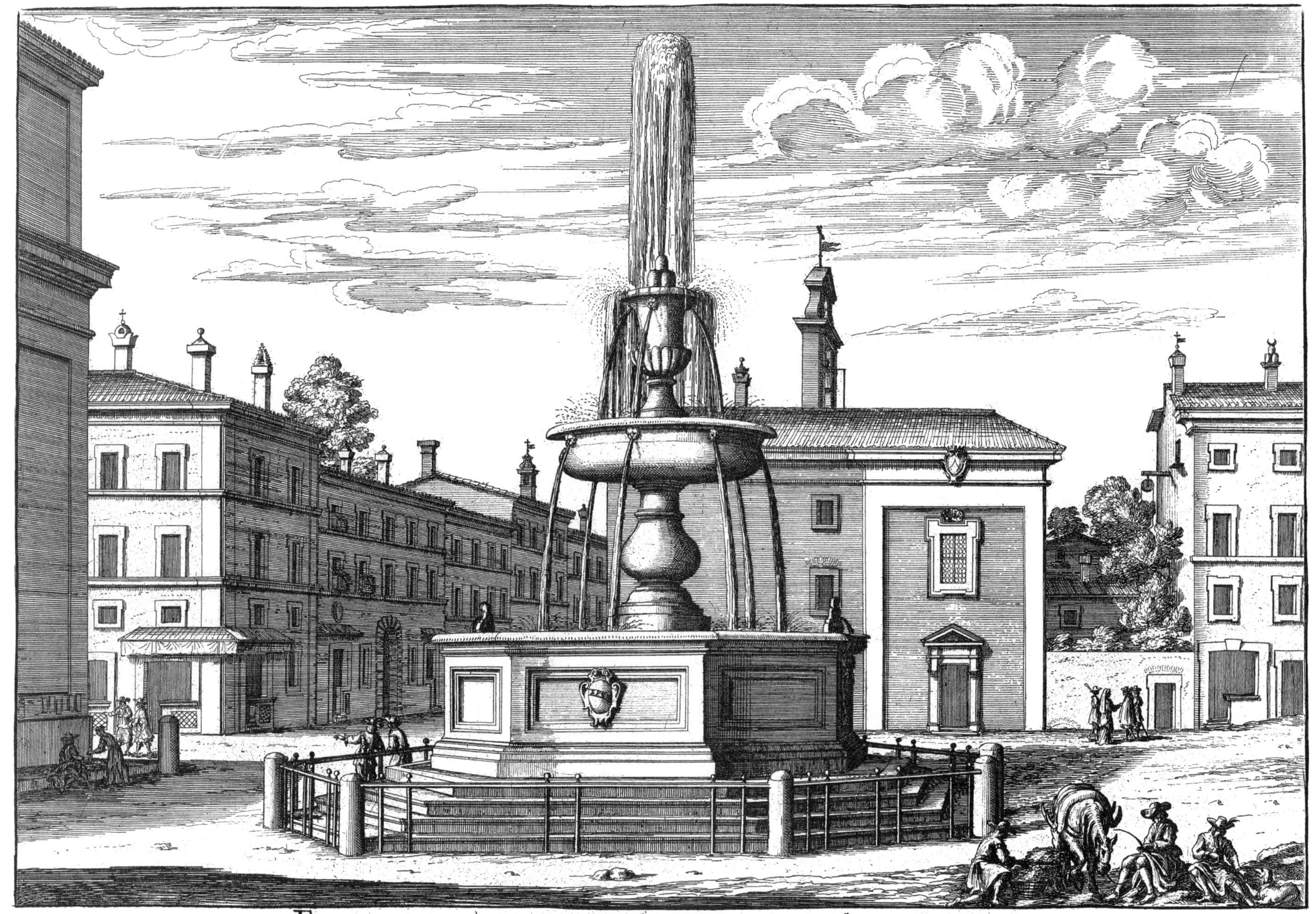

FONTANA SV LA PIAZZA DELLA MAD.ᵃ DE MONTI.
Architetᵃ di Giacomo della Porta.

FOUNTAIN IN PIAZZA MADONNA DEI MONTI. ARCHITECTURE BY GIACOMO DELLA PORTA.

30

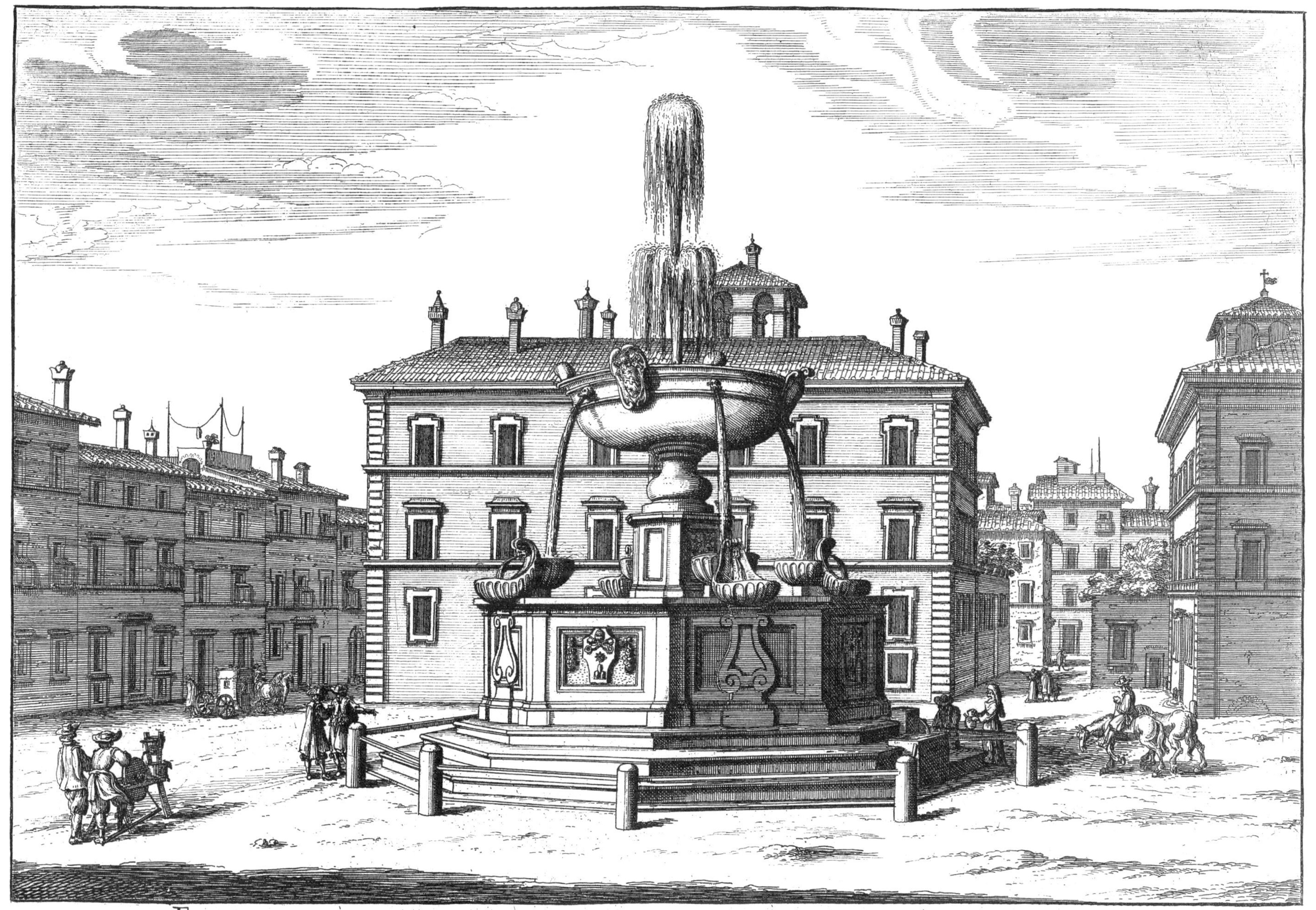

FONTANA SV LA PIAZZA DELLA BASILICA DI S. MARIA IN TRASTEVERE.

Architet.ª di Gio. Fontana, sotto Clem. VIII, riſtorata, e rialzata sotto Aleſſ. VII.

FOUNTAIN IN THE PIAZZA OF THE BASILICA OF OUR LADY IN TRASTEVERE. ARCHITECTURE BY GIOVANNI FONTANA,
RESTORED UNDER CLEMENT VIII, MOUNTED ON STEPS UNDER ALEXANDER VII.

31

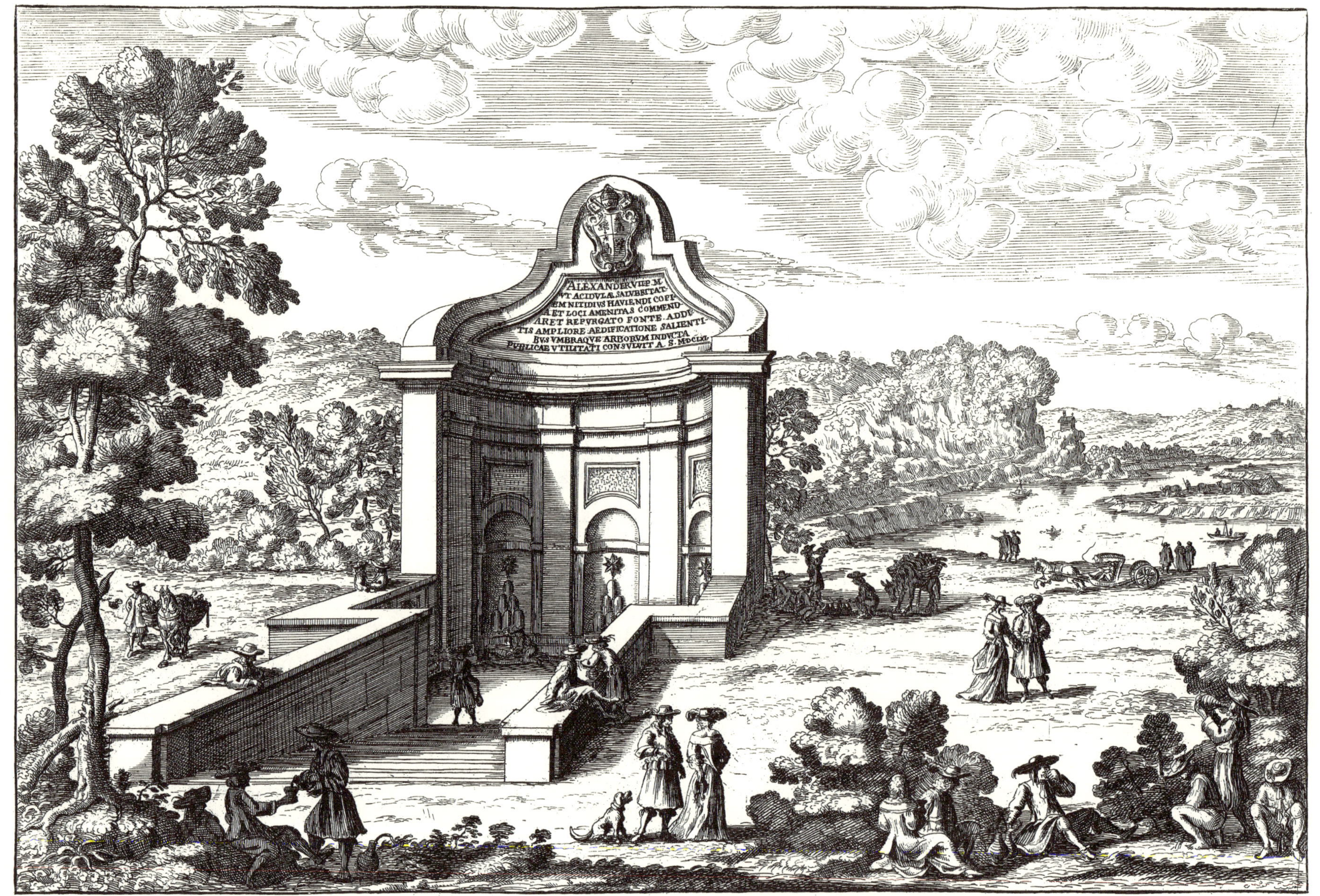

FONTANA CELEBRE D'ACQVA ACETOSA.

fuori la Porta del Popolo, à destra sù la ripa del' Teuere, Architet.ᵃ del Cau. Gio. Lorenzo Bernini, l'acqua è acida, è minerale, e si beue per essere salutifera à molti mali.

FAMOUS FOUNTAIN OF ACQUA ACETOSA, OUTSIDE PORTA DEL POPOLO, ON THE RIGHT BANK OF THE TIBER. ARCHITECTURE BY SIR GIO. LORENZO BERNINI. ITS WATER IS ACIDIC AND MINERAL, AND DRUNK AS A REMEDY TO MANY AILMENTS.

32

LE FONTANE DELLE VILLE

DI FRASCATI, NEL TVSCVLANO,

CON LI LORO PROSPETTI,

PARTE SECONDA,

DISEGNATE, ET INTAGLIATE

DA GIO: BATTISTA FALDA.

Date in luce con direttione, e cura da GIO: GIACOMO DE ROSSI, dalle sue stampe in Roma alla Pace, con Priu. del S. Pont.

FOUNTAINS OF THE FRASCATI VILLAS, IN THE TUSCULUM AREA, AND THEIR FRONTAL VIEWS. PART TWO. DRAWN AND ENGRAVED BY GIO. BATTISTA FALDA. PRINTED, SUPERVISED, AND EDITED BY GIO. GIACOMO DE ROSSI FOR HIS PRESS IN VIA DELLA PACE IN ROME AND WITH THE PATRONAGE OF THE HOLY FATHER.

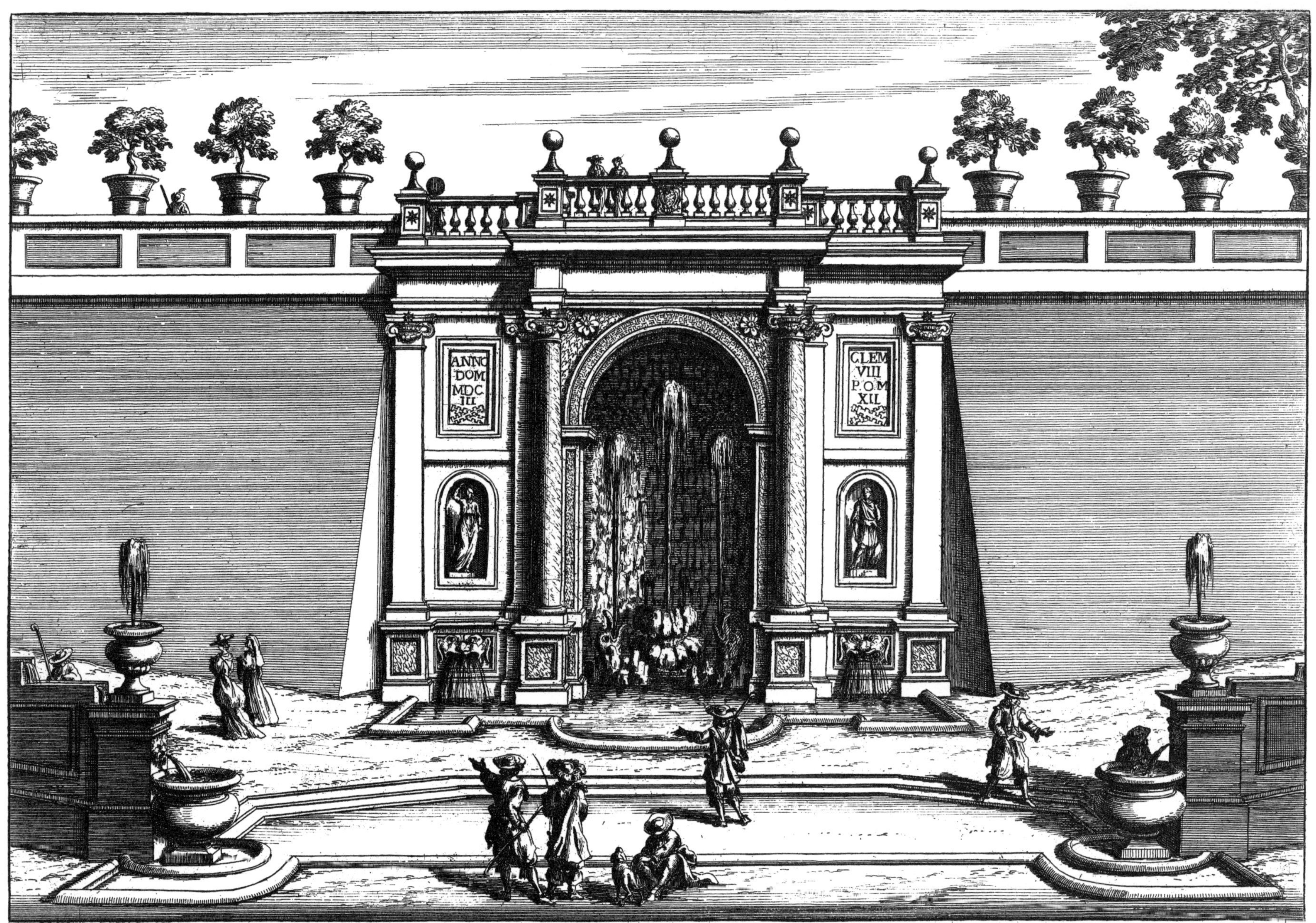

FONTANA, E PROSPETTO SOPRA IL VIALE DE CIPRESSI, NEL PRIMO INGRESSO DELLA VILLA ALDOBRANDINA DI BELVE=
DERE À FRASCATI, ARCHITETTVRA DI GIACOMO DELLA PORTA ARCHITETTO DI TVTTA LA VILLA, CON GIVOCHI D'ACQVE DI
ORATIO OLIVIERI ROMANO.

FOUNTAIN AT THE FIRST ENTRANCE OF VILLA ALDOBRANDINI BELVEDERE IN FRASCATI, AND FRONTAL VIEW ON VIALE DEI CIPRESSI.
ARCHITECTURE BY GIACOMO DELLA PORTA, ARCHITECT OF THE ENTIRE VILLA, WITH WATERWORKS BY ORAZIO OLIVIERI ROMANO.

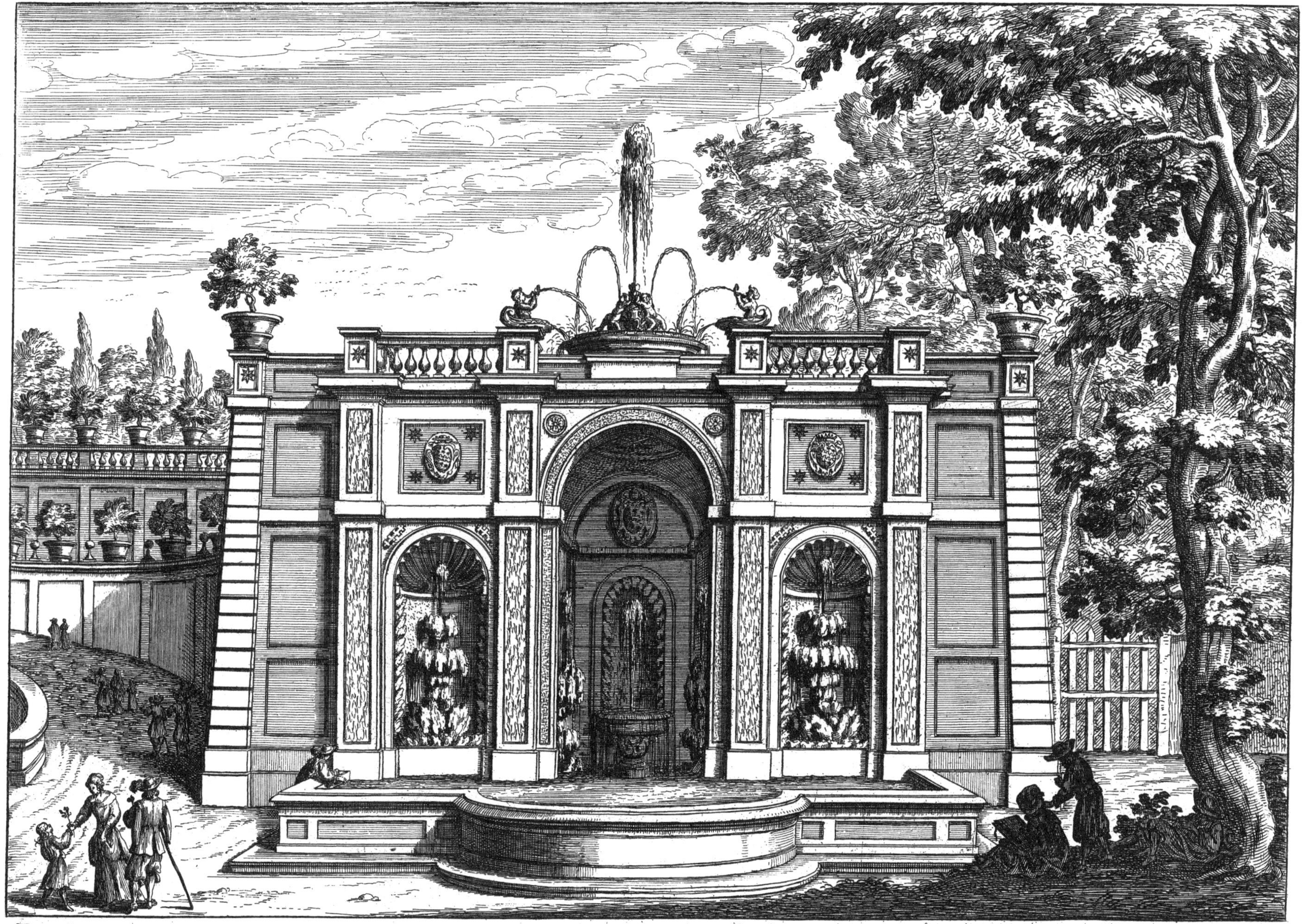

FONTANA NEL SECONDO INGRESSO DVPPLICATA DA I LATI, DI QVA, ET DI LÀ COL MEDESIMO DISEGNO, ET ARCHI-
TETTVRA NELLA SALITA PER ANDARE AL PALAZZO DI BELVEDERE À FRASCATI.

FOUNTAIN AT THE SECOND ENTRANCE, WITH THE SAME DESIGN AND ARCHITECTURE ON BOTH OF ITS SIDES,
LOCATED ON THE ROAD UP TO PALAZZO BELVEDERE IN FRASCATI.

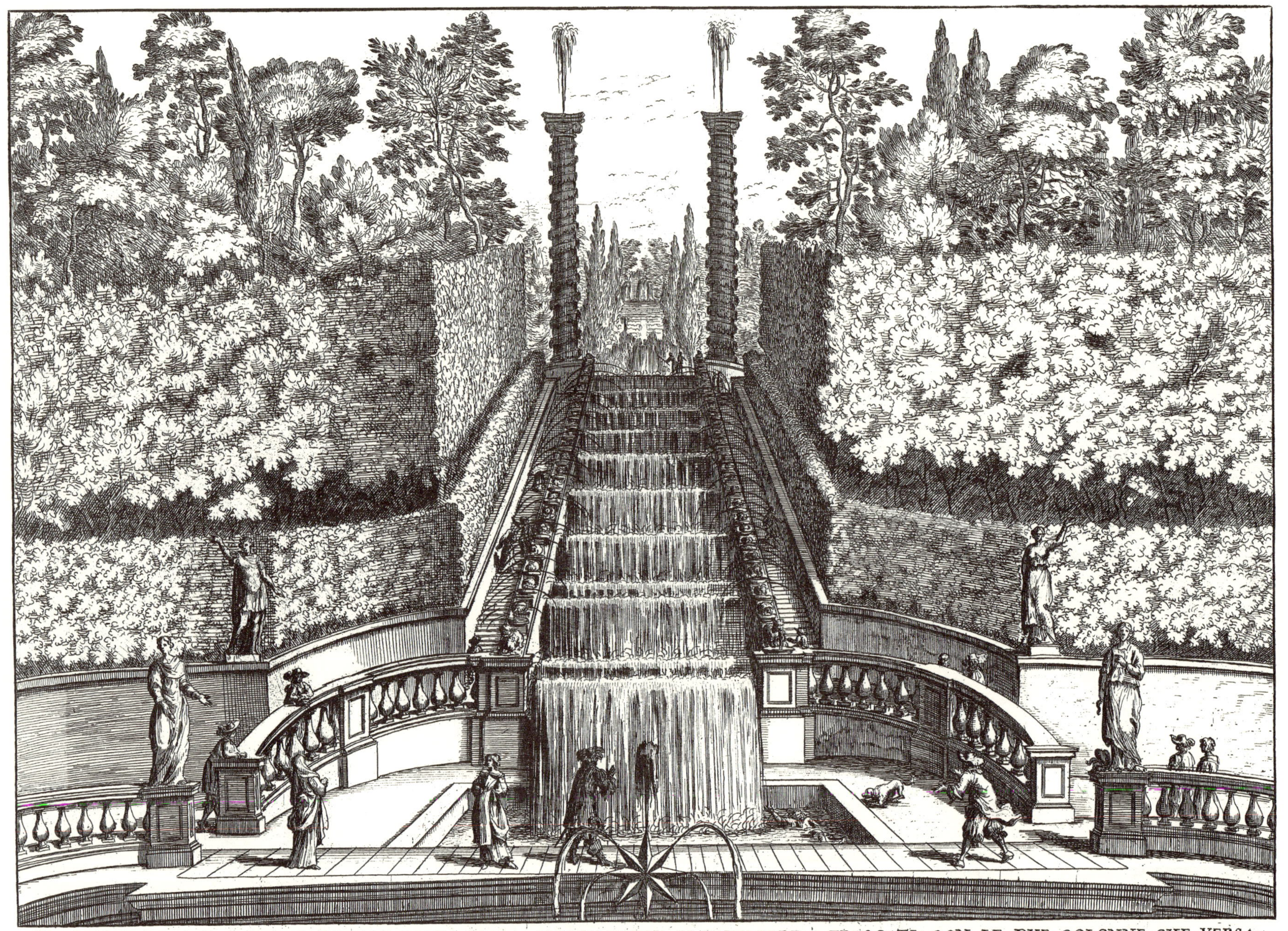

WATERFALL OVER THE THEATER OF VILLA ALDOBRANDINI BELVEDERE IN FRASCATI, WITH TWIN WATER-POURING COLUMNS AT THE TOP, AND VARIOUS WATERWORKS SPLASHING THOSE WHO CLIMB THE STAIRS TO LOOK.

36

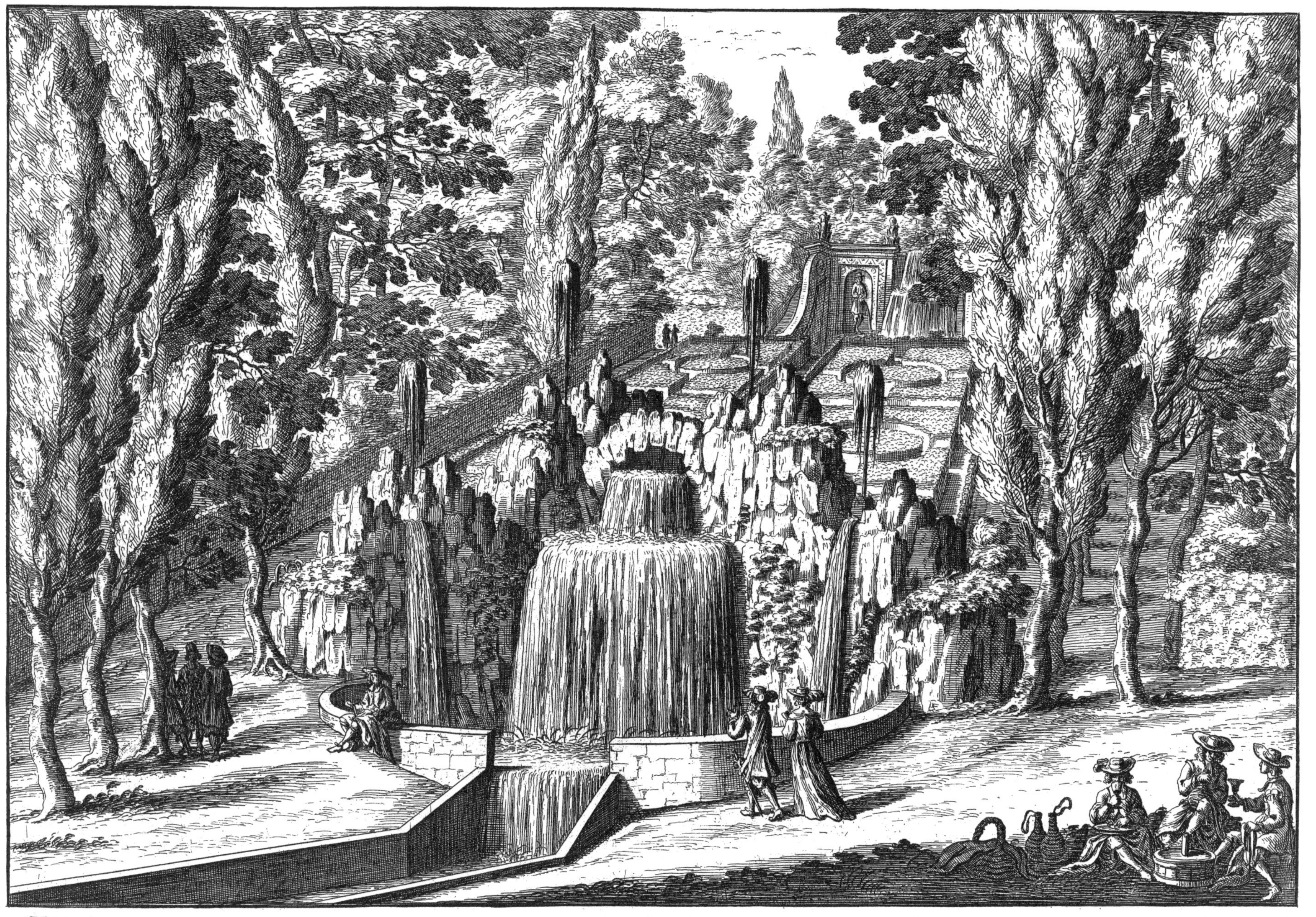

FONTANA RVSTICA NEL PIANO SVPERIORE ALLA CASCATA DEL TEATRO DELLA VILLA ALDOBRANDINA DI BELVEDERE A FRASCATI.

RUSTIC FOUNTAIN ON THE UPPER LEVEL OF THE THEATER WATERFALL OF VILLA ALDOBRANDINI BELVEDERE IN FRASCATI.

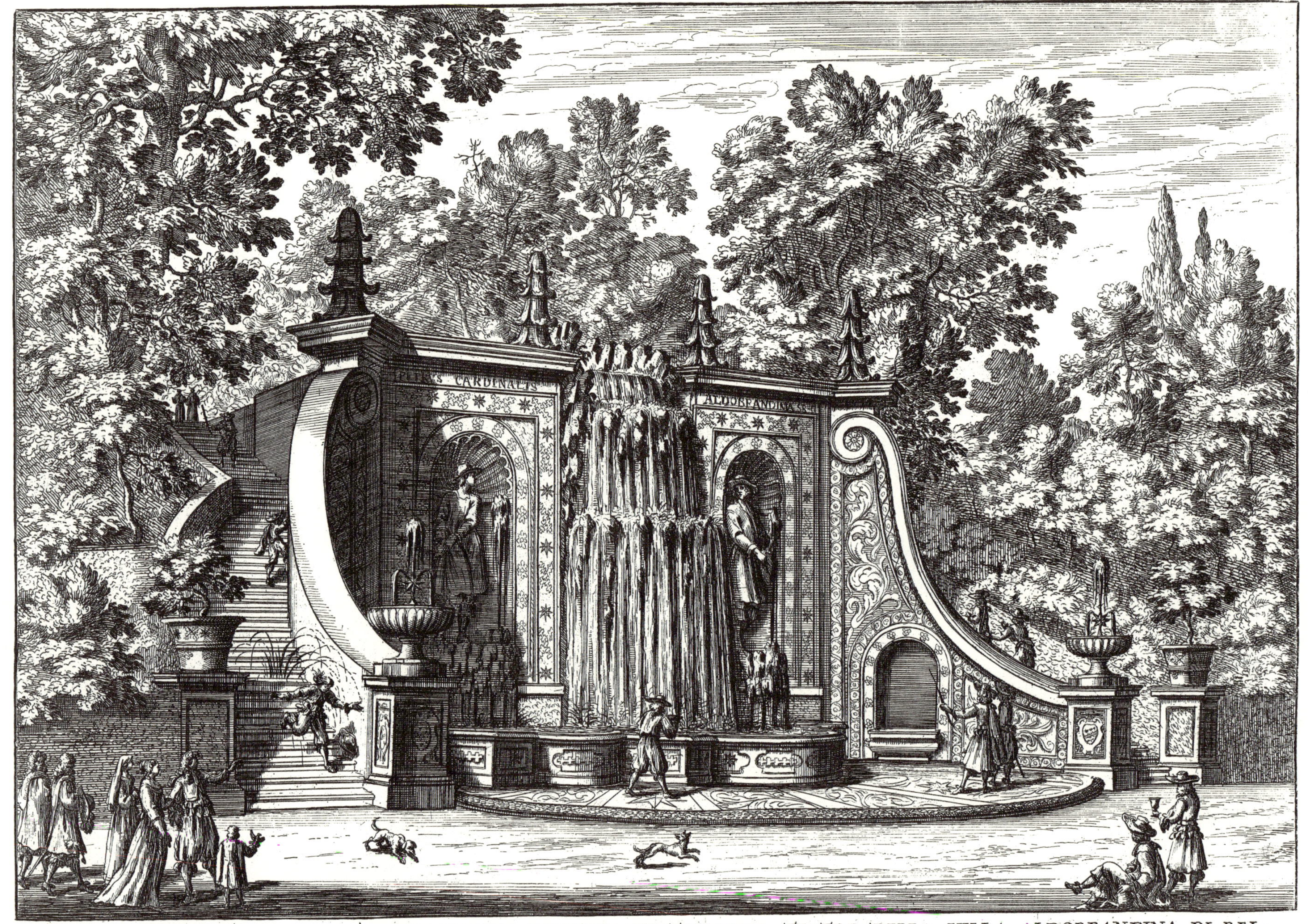

ALTRA FONTANA PIV SOPRA ALL'ANTECEDENTE FONTANA RVSTICA DEL TEATRO DELLA VILLA ALDOBRANDINA DI BEL-
VEDERE A FRASCATI, CON GIVOCHI D'ACQVE NELLE SCALE.

ANOTHER FOUNTAIN IN VILLA ALDOBRANDINI BELVEDERE IN FRASCATI, ABOVE THE PREVIOUS RUSTIC FOUNTAIN OF THE THEATER,
WITH WATERWORKS EMBEDDED IN ITS STAIRS.

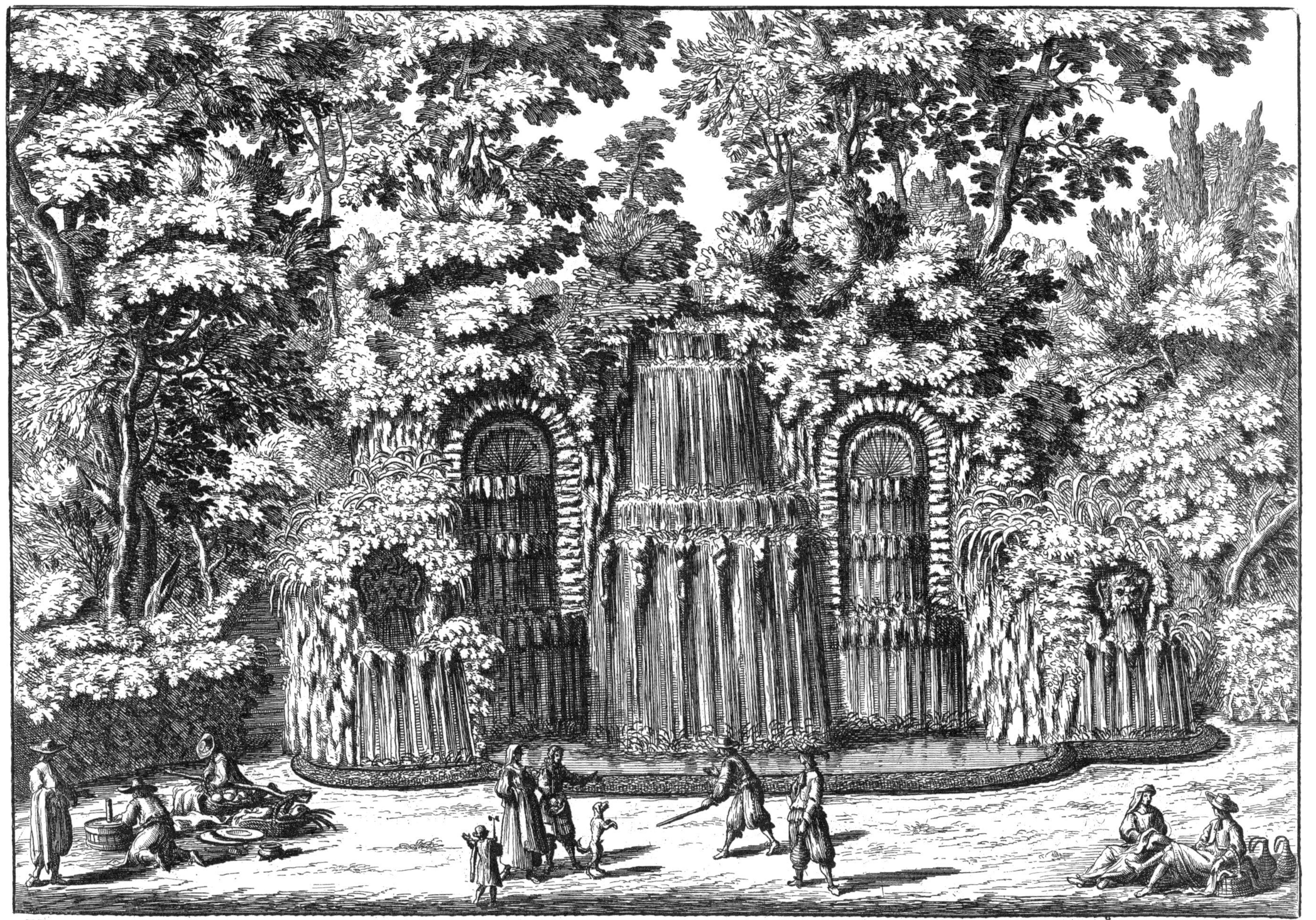

VLTIMO PROSPETTO DI FONTANE DEL TEATRO DELLA VILLA ALDOBRANDINA DI BELVEDERE A FRASCATI, NEL=
LA SOMMITÀ PIV ALTA DEL MONTE, DOVE L'ACQVA ALGIDA FÀ LA PRIMA MOSTRA, DERIVANDO DA GLI ACQVEDOTTI
PER SPATIO DI SEI MIGLIA.

LAST FRONTAL VIEW OF FOUNTAINS IN THE THEATER OF VILLA ALDOBRANDINI BELVEDERE IN FRASCATI, ATOP THE HILL,
WHERE THE ICY WATER FIRST FLOWS FROM AQUEDUCTS SIX MILES AWAY.

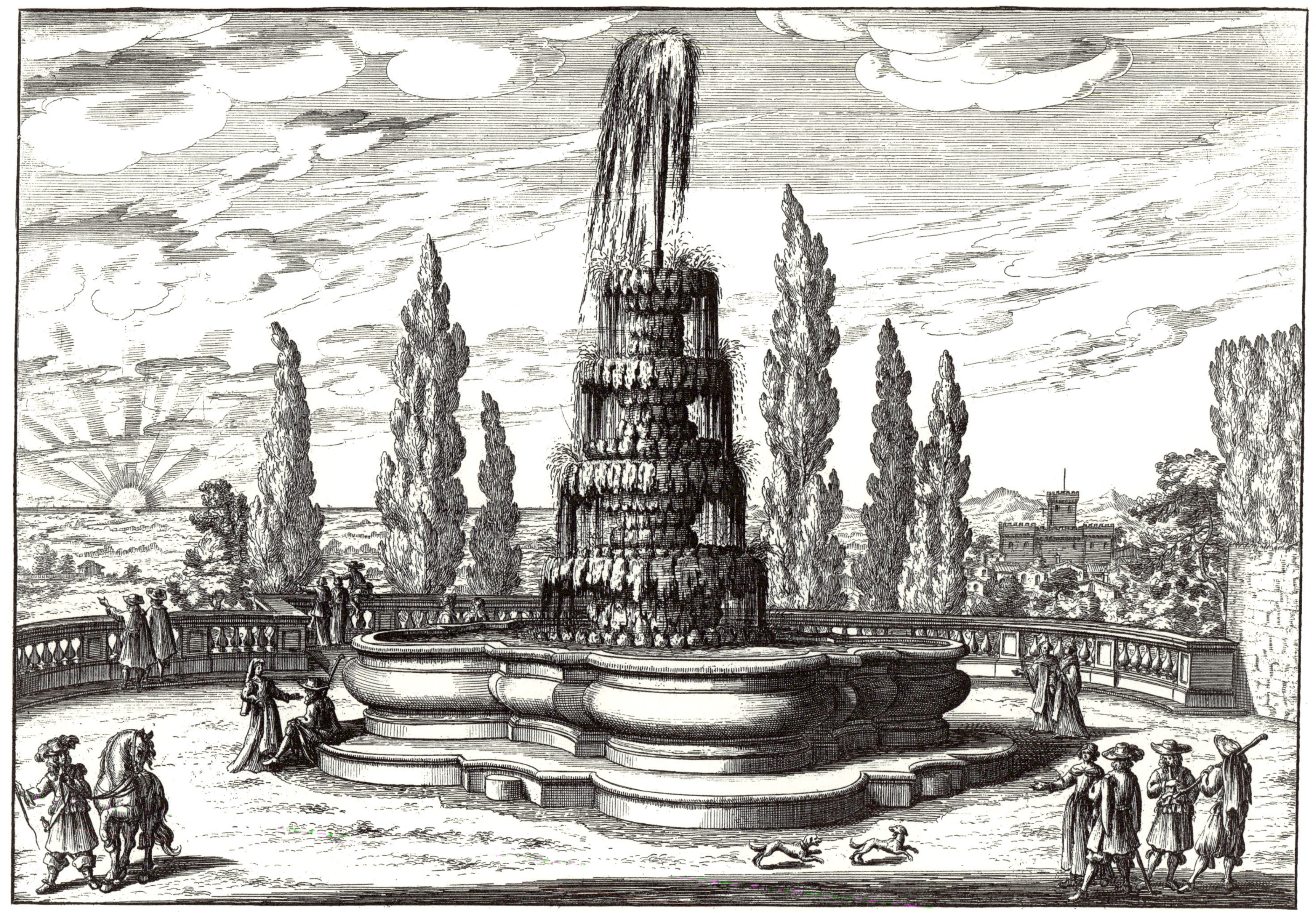

PRIMA FONTANA AVANTI IL PALAZZO DEL GIARDINO LVDOVISI À FRASCATI.

FIRST FOUNTAIN IN FRONT OF THE PALACE OF THE GIARDINO LUDOVISI IN FRASCATI.

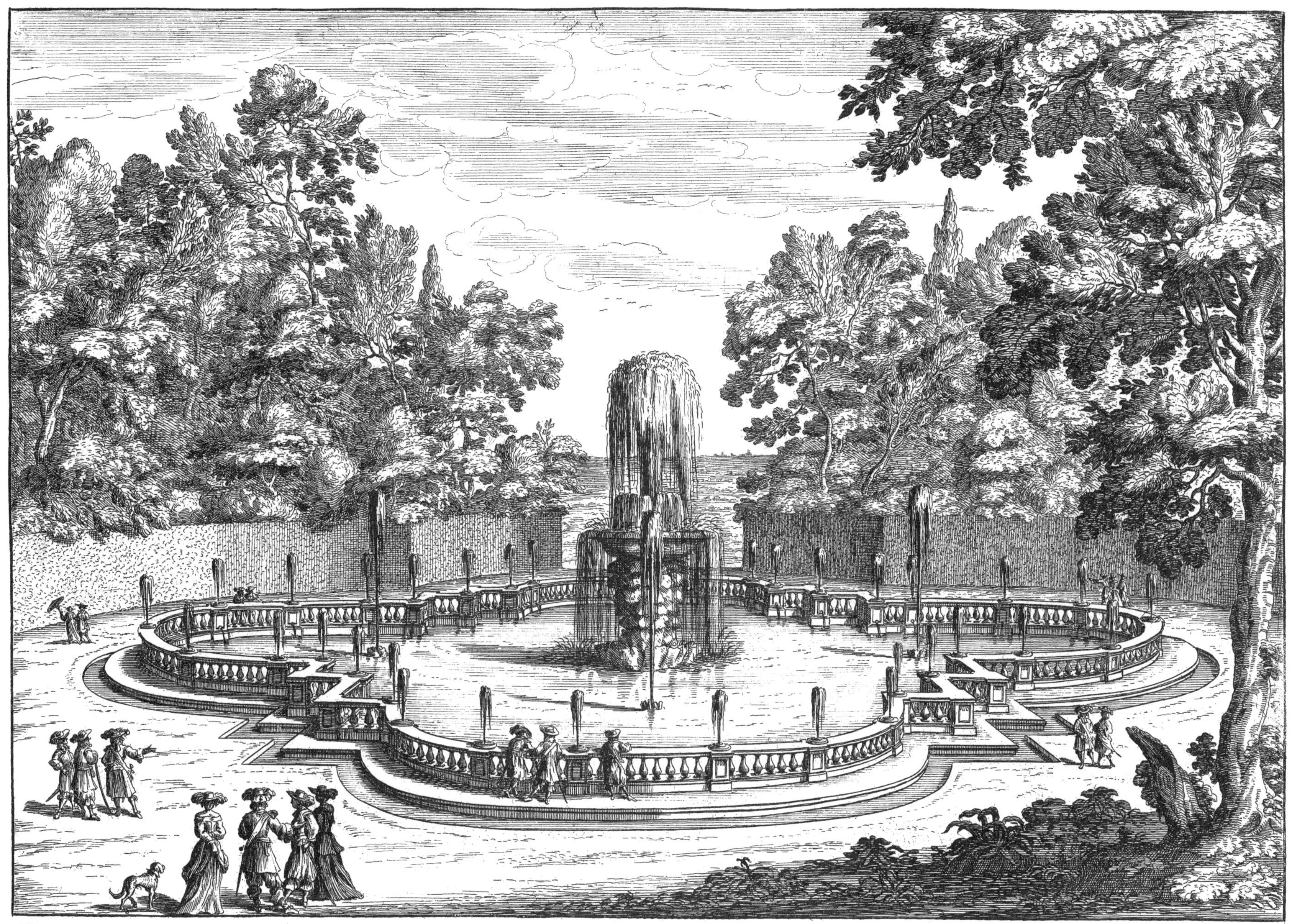

UPPER FOUNTAIN, ATOP THE STAIRS, AND WATERFALL ABOVE THE THEATER IN THE WOODS OF THE GIARDINO LUDOVISI IN FRASCATI.

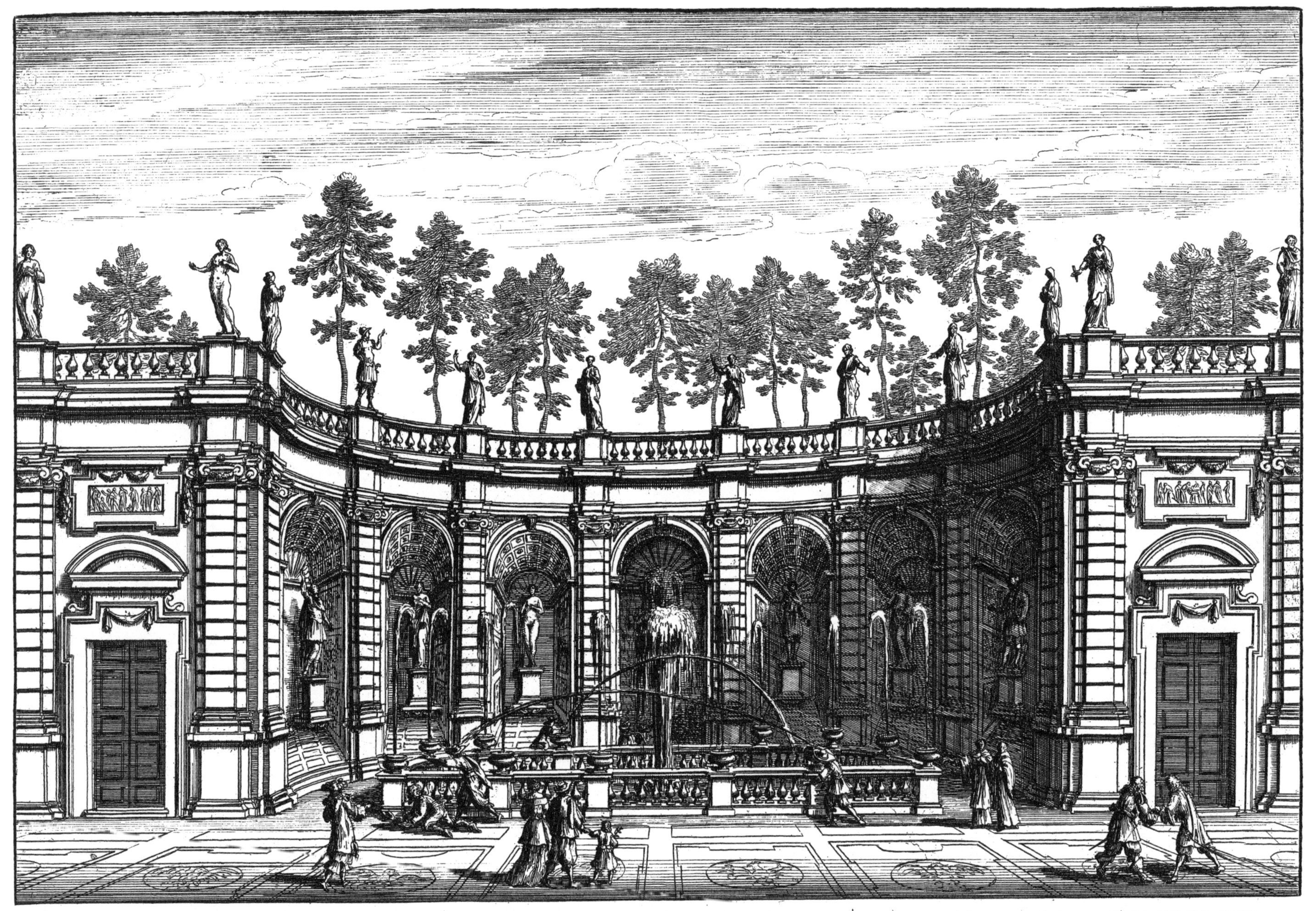

TEATRO DELLE FONTANE DELLA VILLA BORGHESE DI MONDRAGONE À FRASCATI CON DIVERSI GIVOCHI D'ACQVE ARCHITETTVRA DI GIOVANNI FONTANA.

FOUNTAIN THEATER OF VILLA MONDRAGONE BORGHESE IN FRASCATI WITH VARIOUS WATERWORKS. ARCHITECTURE BY GIOVANNI FONTANA.

42

LE · FONTANE ·
NE' · PALAZZI · E · NE' · GIARDINI DI · ROMA ·
CON · LI · LORO · PROSPETTI · ET · ORNAMENTI

DISEGNATE · ED · INTAGLIATE ·
DA · GIO · FRANCESCO · VENTVRINI ·

PARTE TERZA ·

Data in luce con direttione, e cura di Gio · Giacomo de Rossi, nella sua staperia

in Roma, alla Pace, all' Insegna di Parigi, con Priu. del' S. Pont.

FOUNTAINS IN PALACES AND GARDENS OF ROME, THEIR FRONTAL VIEWS AND ORNAMENTS. DRAWN AND ENGRAVED BY GIO. FRANCESCO VENTURINI. PART THREE. PRINTED, SUPERVISED, AND EDITED BY GIO. GIACOMO DE ROSSI FOR HIS PRESS IN VIA DELLA PACE IN ROME, BY THE PARIGI SIGN, AND WITH THE PATRONAGE OF THE HOLY FATHER.

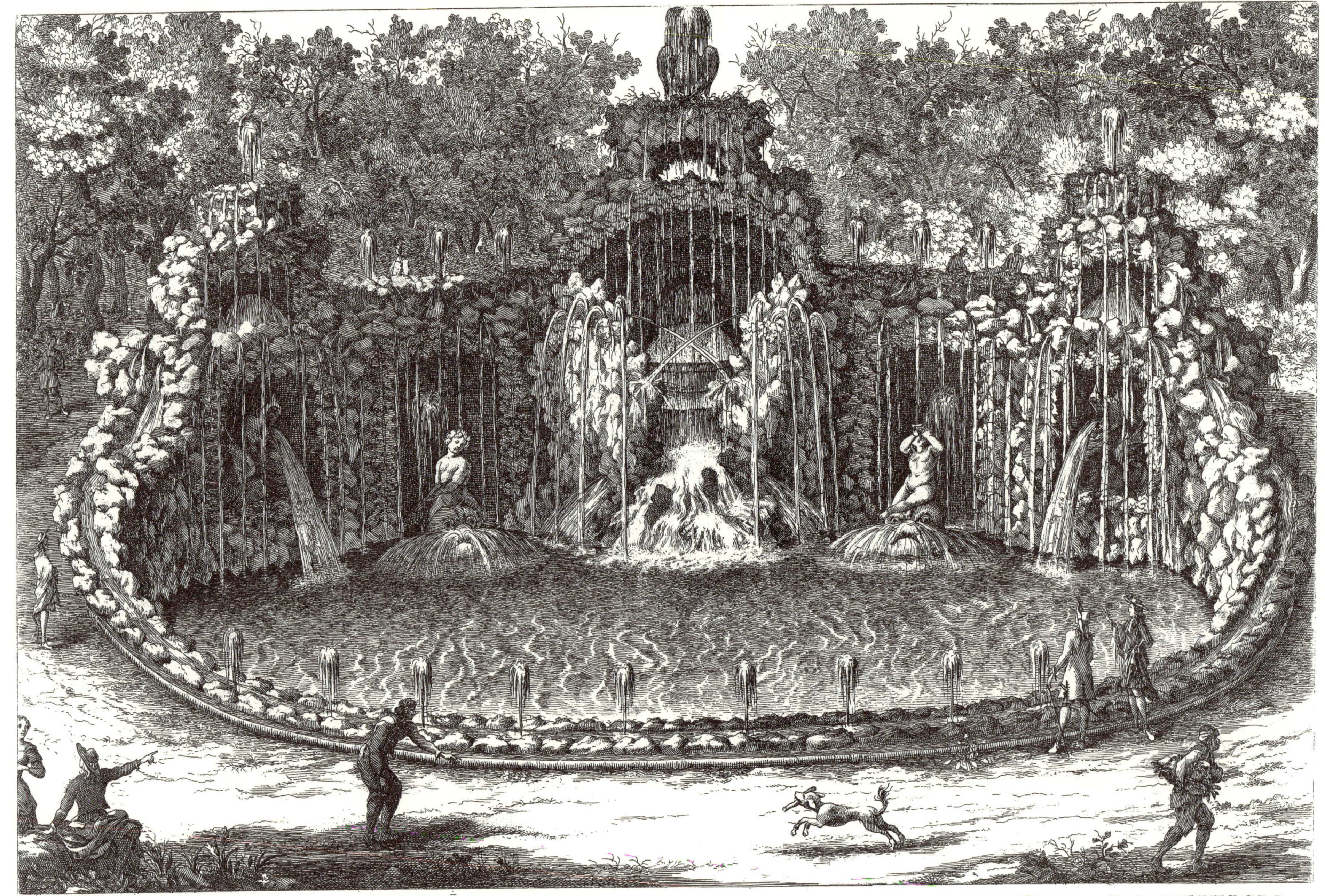

FONTANA DETTA LO SCOGLIO NEL GIARDINO DI BELVEDERE NEL PALAZZO PONTIFICIO

FOUNTAIN KNOWN AS THE ROCK, IN THE BELVEDERE GARDEN OF THE VATICAN PALACE. ARCHITECTURE BY CARLO MADERNO.

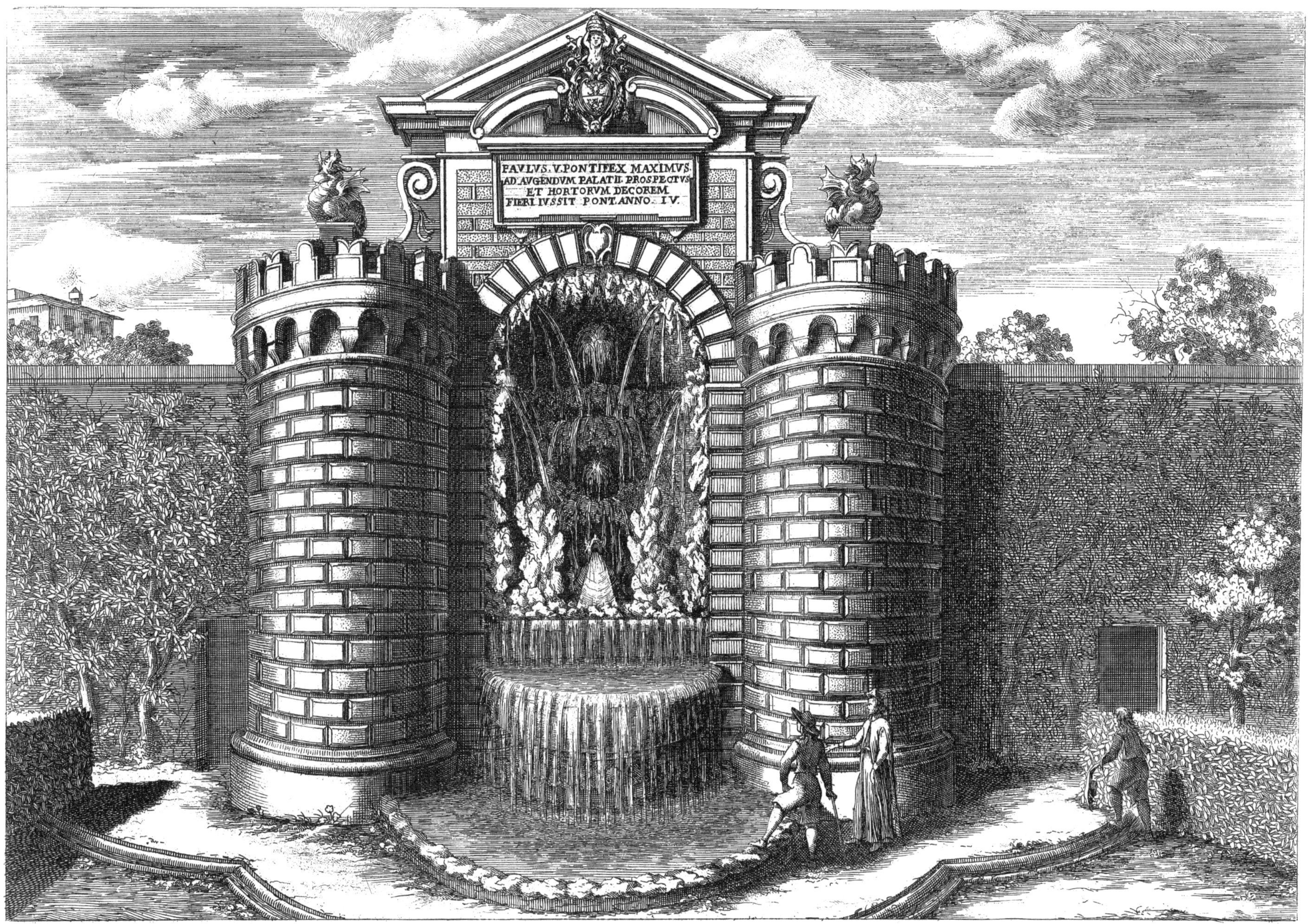

FONTANA DELLA TORRE NEL GIARDINO DI BELVEDERE NEL PALAZZO PONTIFICIO

in Vaticano. Architettura di Carlo Maderno.

FOUNTAIN OF THE TOWER, IN THE BELVEDERE GARDEN OF THE VATICAN PALACE. ARCHITECTURE BY CARLO MADERNO.

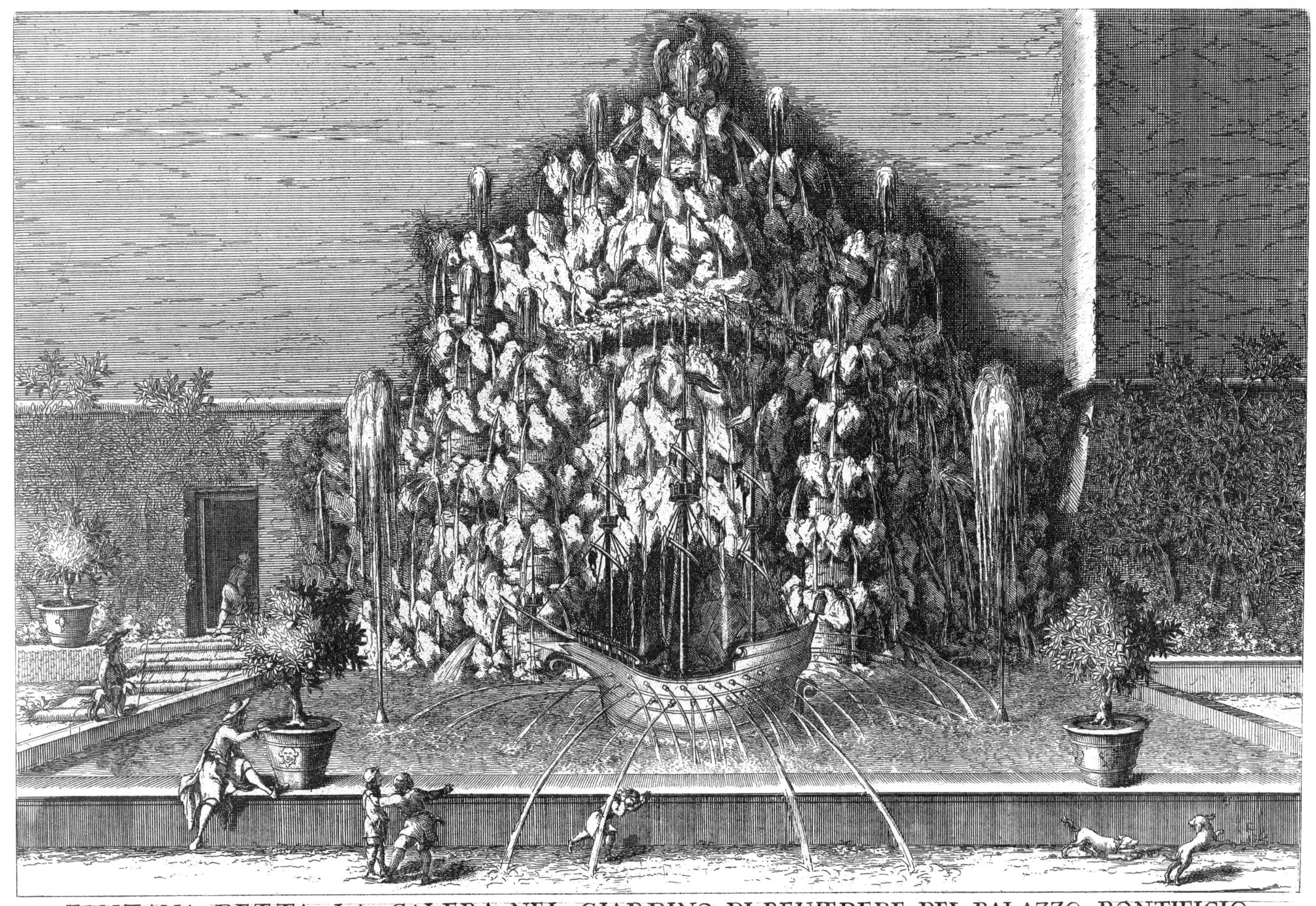

FONTANA DETTA LA GALERA NEL GIARDINO DI BELVEDERE DEL PALAZZO PONTIFICIO
in Vaticano. Architettura di Carlo maderno

FOUNTAIN KNOWN AS THE GALLEY, IN THE BELVEDERE GARDEN OF THE VATICAN PALACE. ARCHITECTURE BY CARLO MADERNO.

46

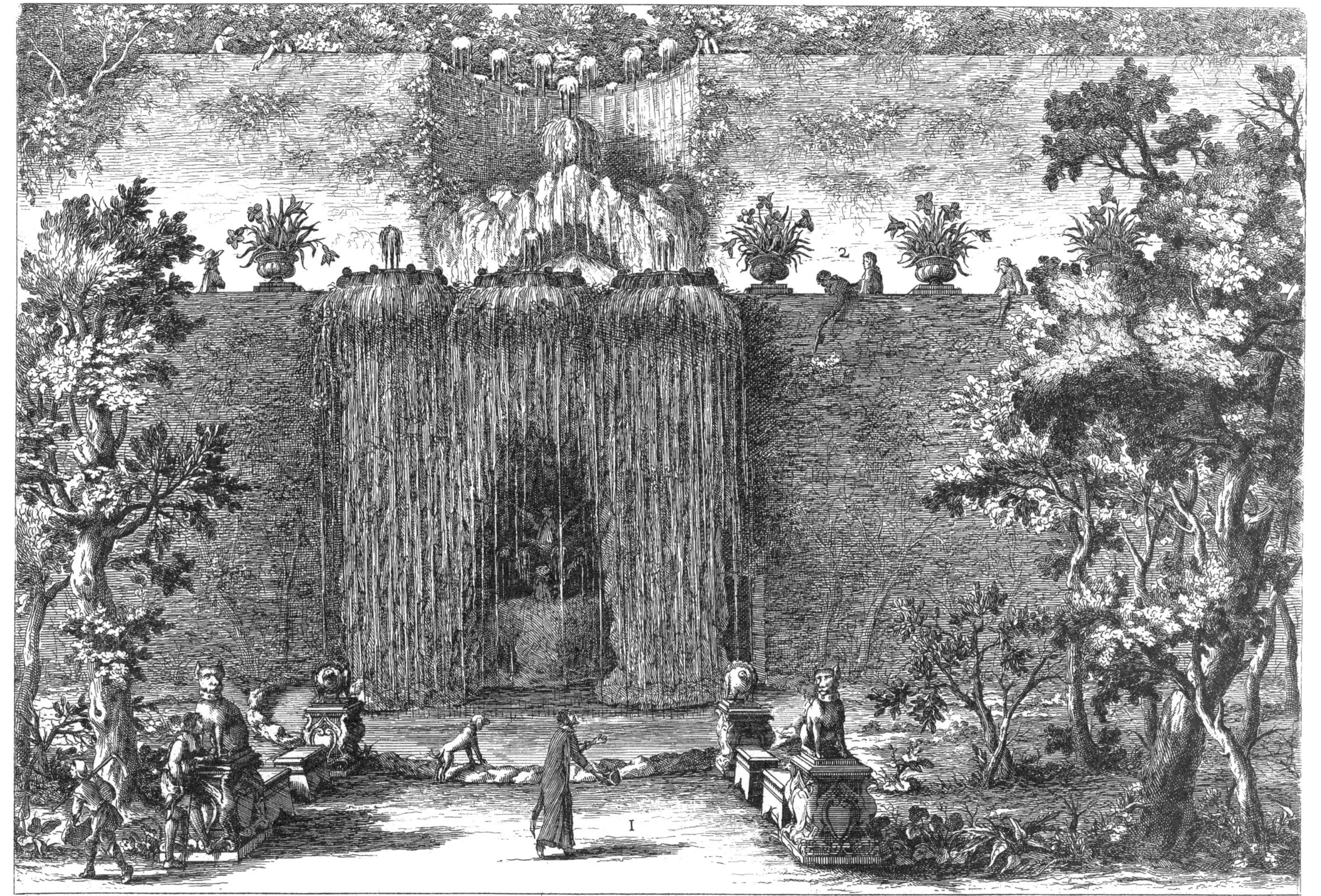

FONTANA DETTA DELLA PIOGGIA NEL GIARDINO DEL PALAZZO PONTIFICIO SVL QVIRINALE
a monte Cauallo nel. primo piano.
ALTRA VEDVTA E PIOGGIA DELLA FONTANA SVLA RVPE SVPERIORE NEL SECONDO PIANO
Architettura di Carlo maderno.

FOUNTAIN KNOWN AS FOUNTAIN OF THE RAIN, IN THE GARDEN OF THE PAPAL PALACE ON THE QUIRINAL HILL, IN THE FOREGROUND, AS SEEN FROM MONTE CAVALLO. IN THE BACKGROUND, ALTERNATE VIEW OF THE FOUNTAIN AND ITS WATERFALL ON THE UPPER CLIFF. ARCHITECTURE BY CARLO MADERNO.

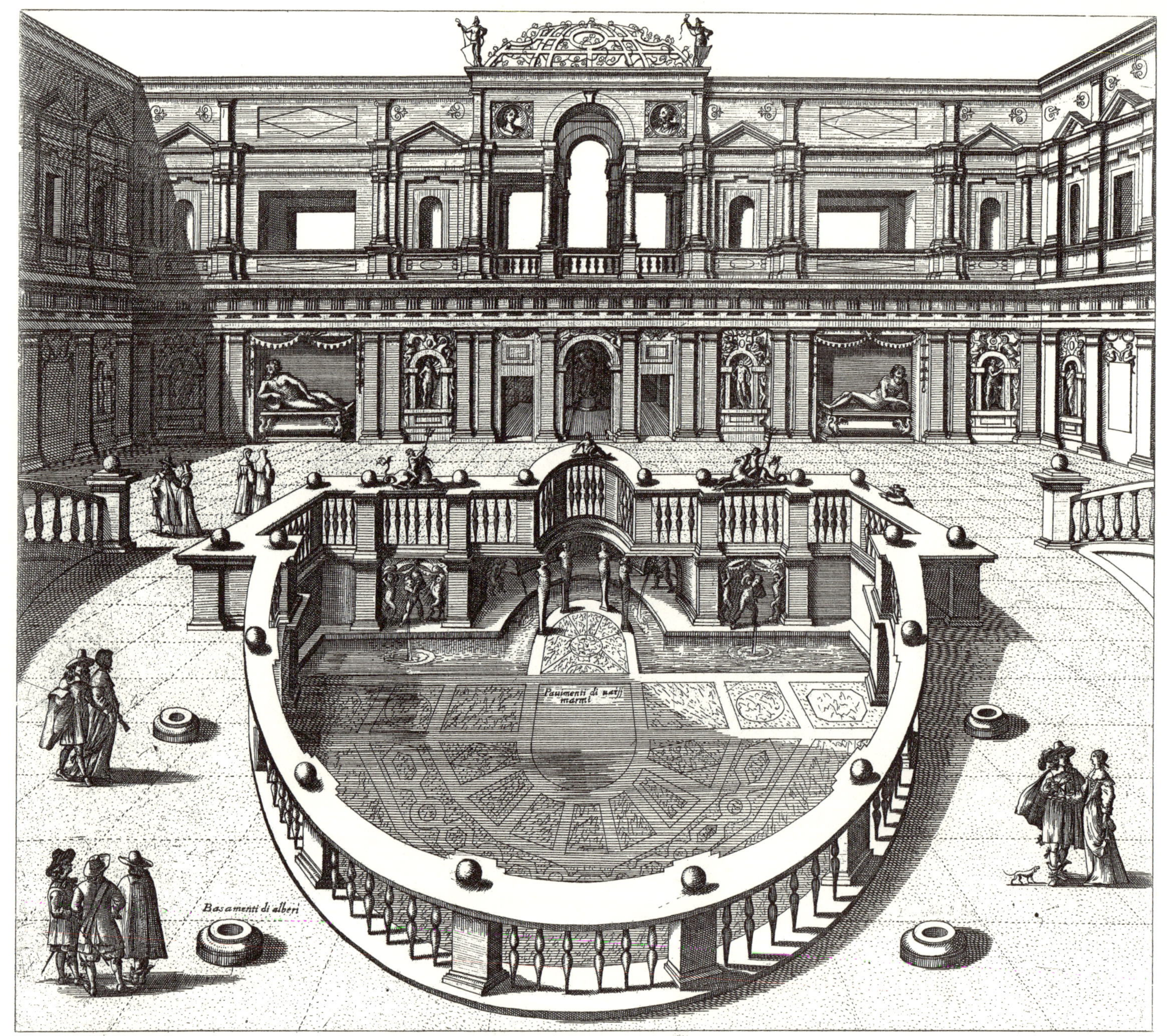

FONTANA FATTA DA PAPA IIVLIO TERZO IN ROMA NELLA VIA FLAMINIA PER ABBELLIMENTO DELLA SVA VIGNA

FOUNTAIN IN VIA FLAMINIA BUILT BY POPE JULIUS III TO EMBELLISH HIS VINEYARD.

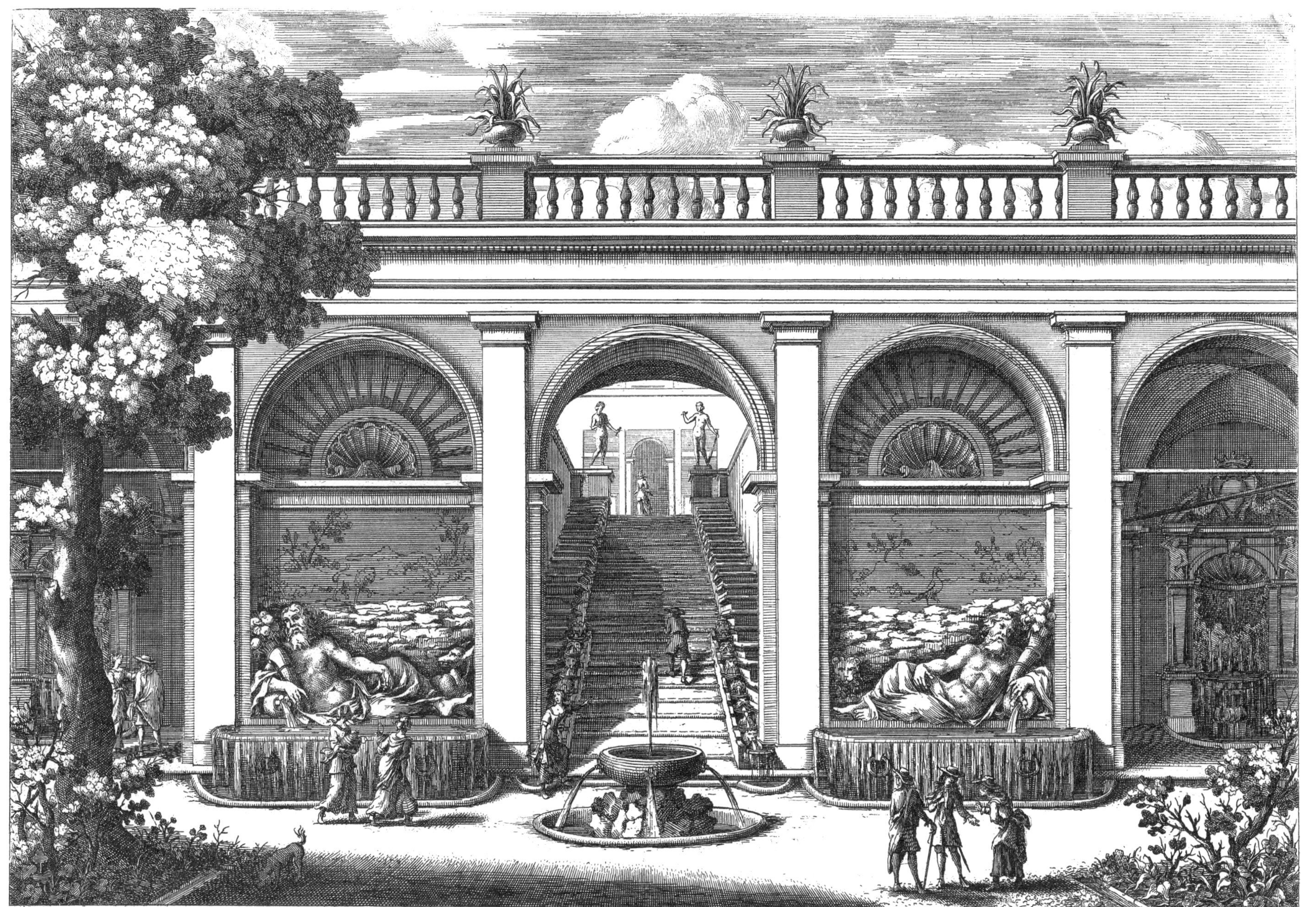

FRONTAL VIEW OF THE FOUNTAINS IN THE GARDEN OF THE BORROMEI OUTSIDE PORTA DEL POPOLO IN VIA FLAMINIA.
ARCHITECTURE BY GIACOMO BAROZZI DA VIGNOLA.

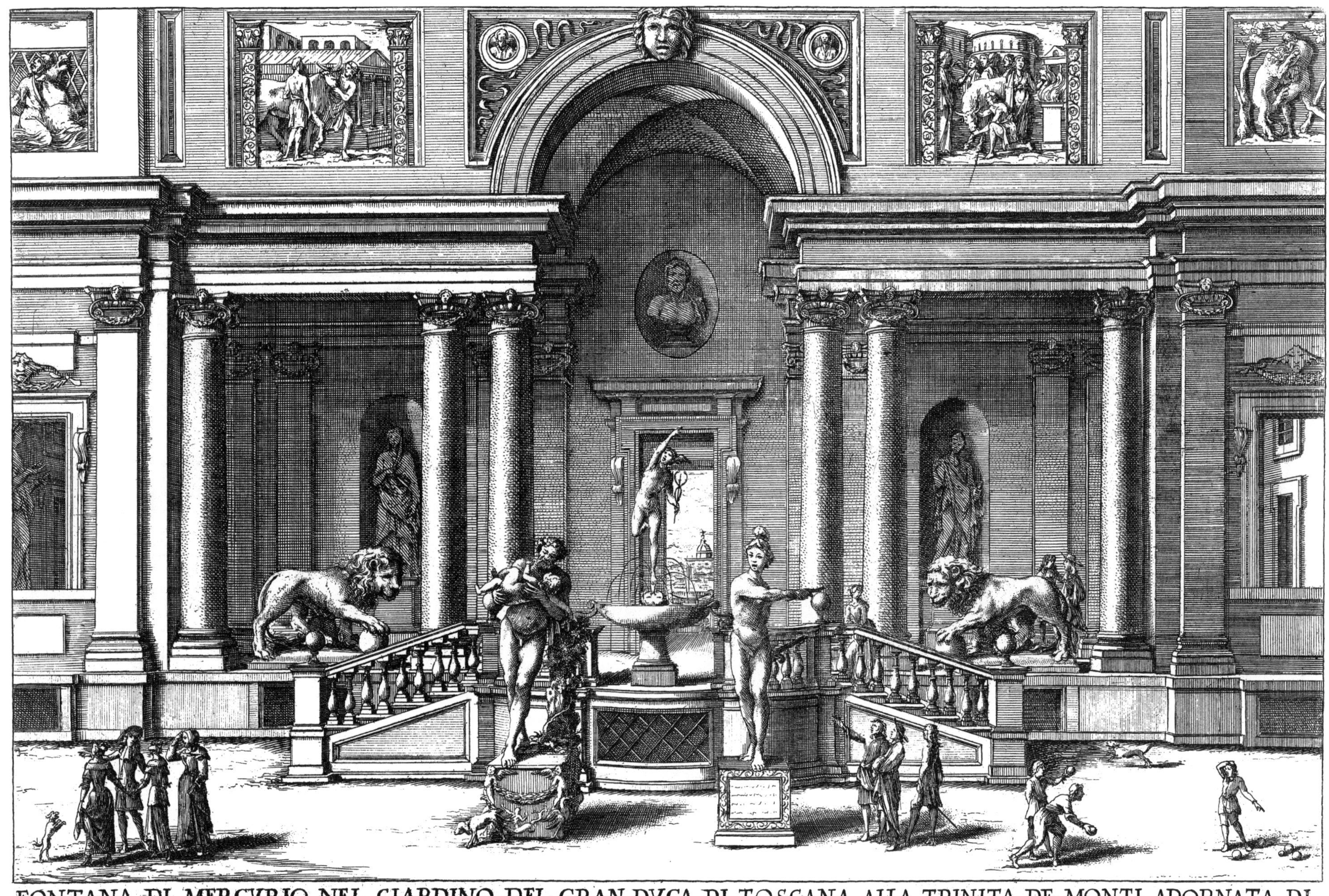

FONTANA DI MERCVRIO NEL GIARDINO DEL GRAN DVCA DI TOSCANA ALLA TRINITA DE MONTI ADORNATA DI STATVE DI METALLO AVANTI IL PORTICO DELLA FACCIATA INTERIORE DEL PALAZZO. *Architettura di Annibale Lippi.*

FOUNTAIN OF MERCURY IN THE GARDEN OF THE GRAND DUKE OF TUSCANY AT TRINITÀ DEI MONTI, ADORNED WITH METAL STATUES, FACING THE PORTICO OF THE INTERNAL FAÇADE OF THE PALACE. ARCHITECTURE BY ANNIBALE LIPPI.

50

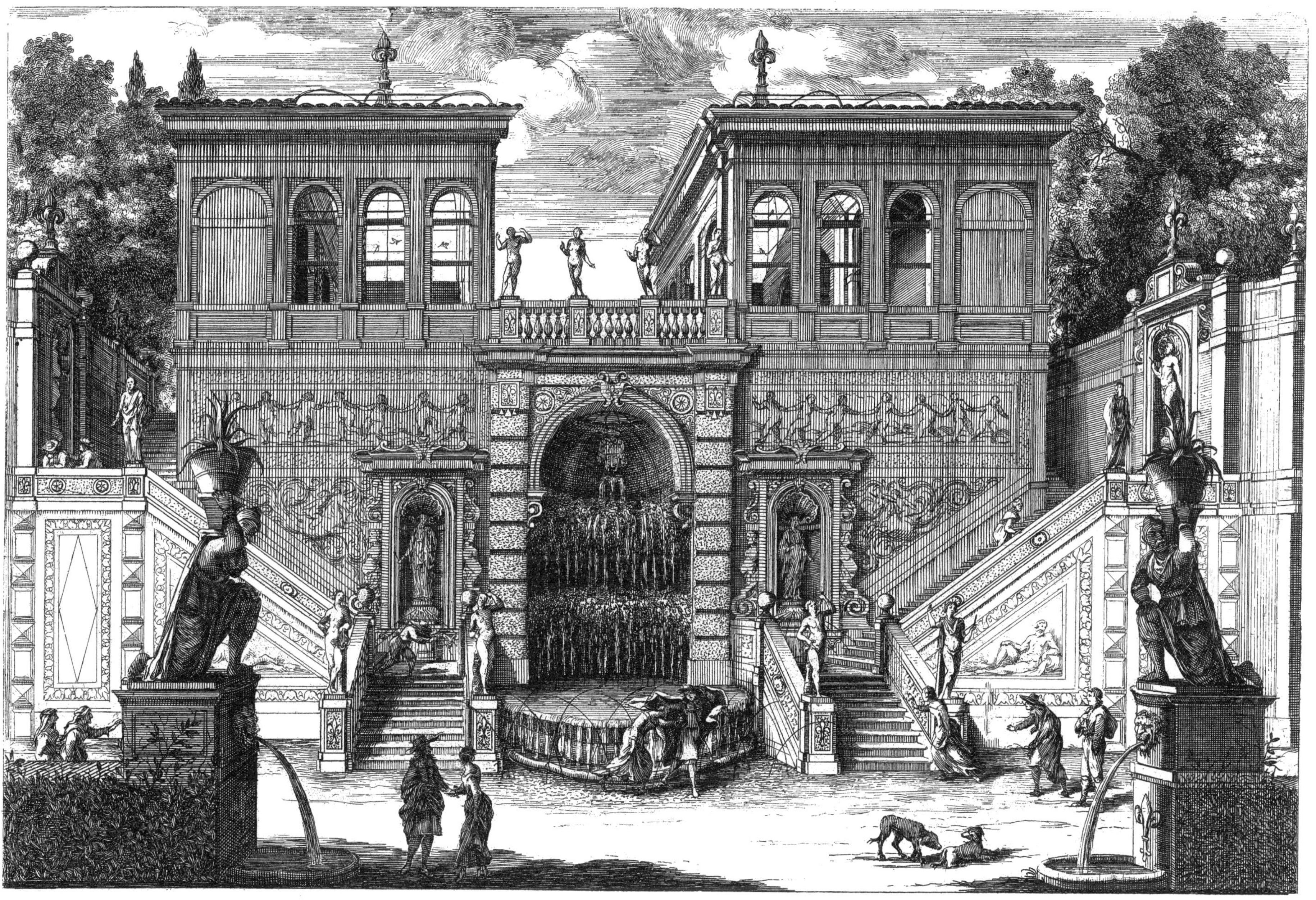

FONTANA E PROSPETTO DEL GIARDINO DEL SIGNOR DVCA DI PARMA

in Campo Vaccino situato sul monte Palatino Architettura del Caualier Girolamo Rainaldi.

FOUNTAIN AND FRONTAL VIEW OF THE GARDEN OF THE DUKE OF PARMA IN CAMPO VACCINO ON THE PALATINE HILL.
ARCHITECTURE BY SIR GIROLAMO RAINALDI.

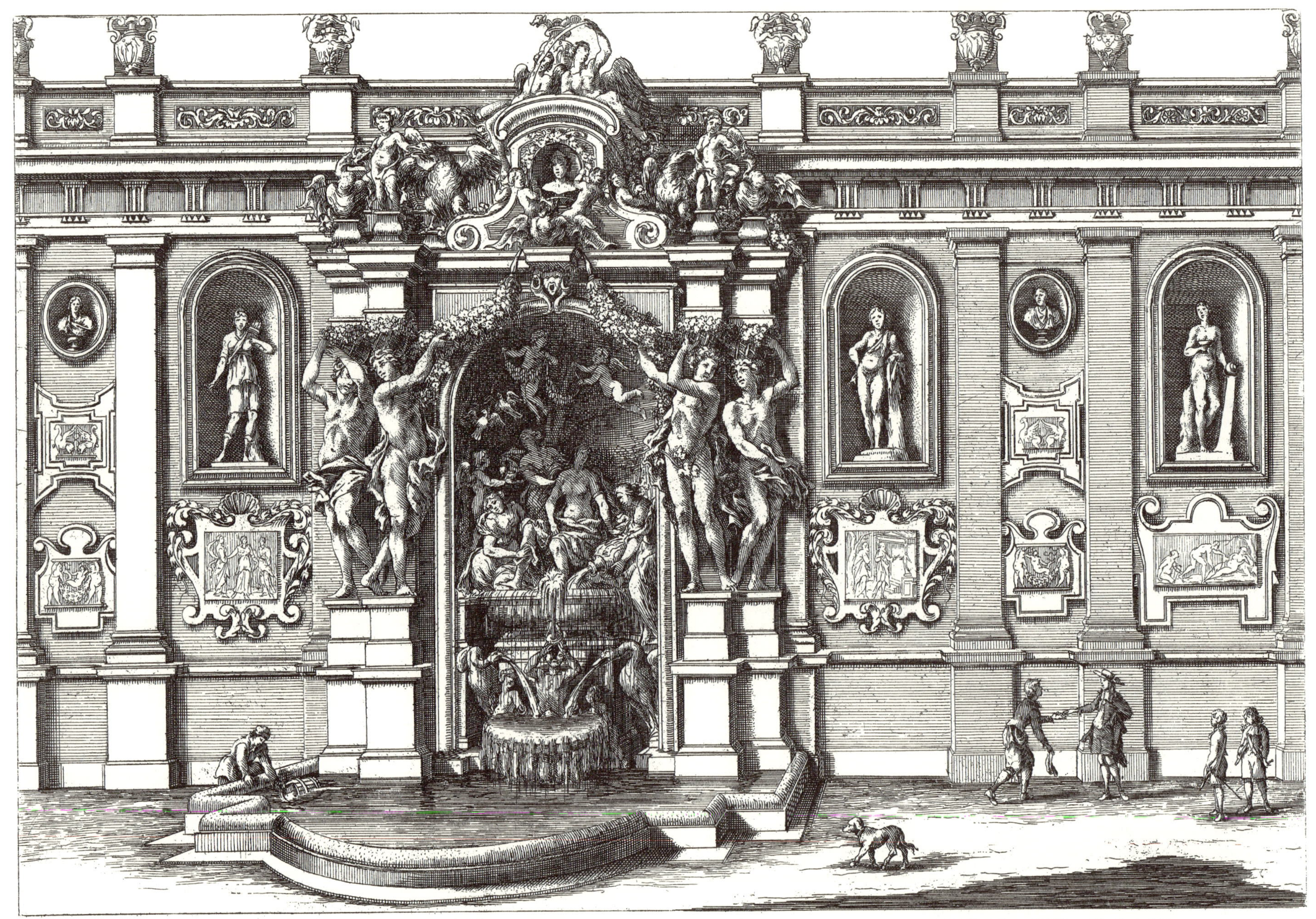

FONTANA NEL PALAZZO DEL SIGNOR PRENCIPE BORGHESE IN ROMA.
situata da un lato del Teatro et Giardino. Architettura del Cau: Carlo Rainaldi.

FOUNTAIN IN THE PALACE OF PRINCE BORGHESE IN ROME, LOCATED ON ONE SIDE OF THE THEATER AND GARDEN.
ARCHITECTURE BY SIR CARLO RAINALDI.

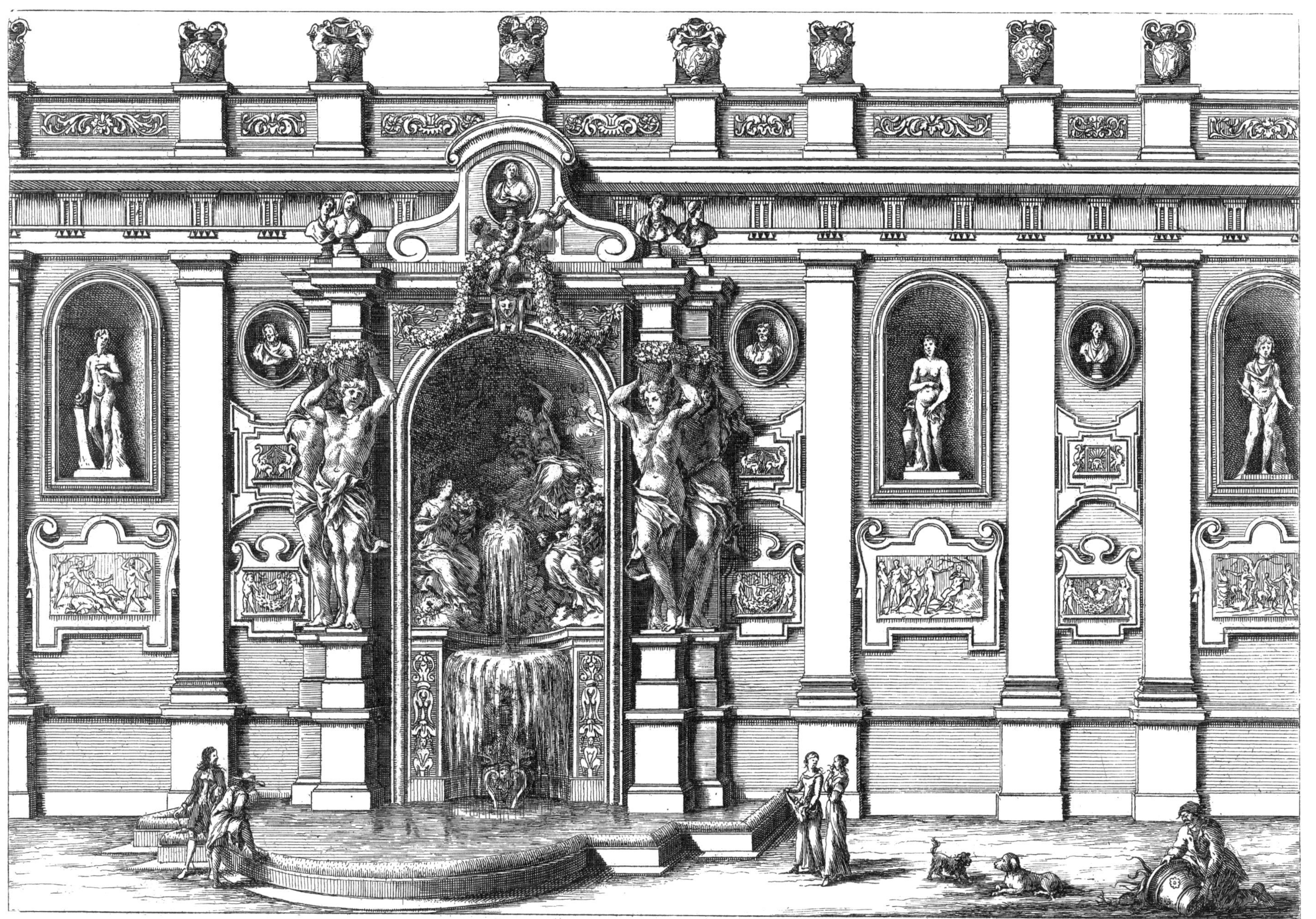

FOUNTAIN IN THE PALACE OF PRINCE BORGHESE IN ROME, FACING THE ENTRANCE OF THE THEATER AND GARDEN. ARCHITECTURE BY SIR CARLO RAINALDI.

53

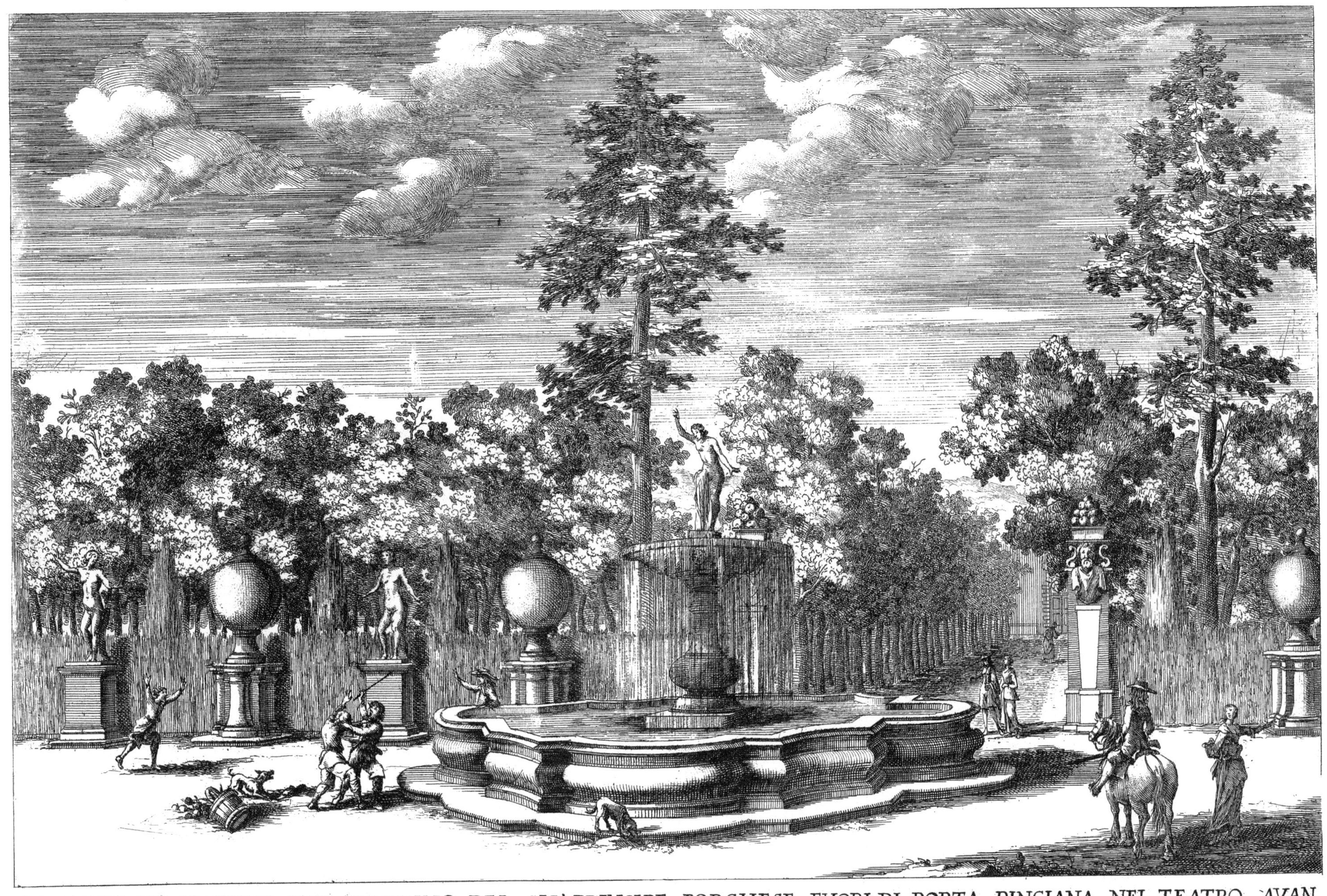

FOUNTAIN OF NARCISSUS IN THE GARDEN OF PRINCE BORGHESE OUTSIDE PORTA PINCIANA, IN THE THEATER FACING THE EASTERN FAÇADE
OF THE PALACE. ARCHITECTURE BY GIO. ANTONIO VANSANTIO.

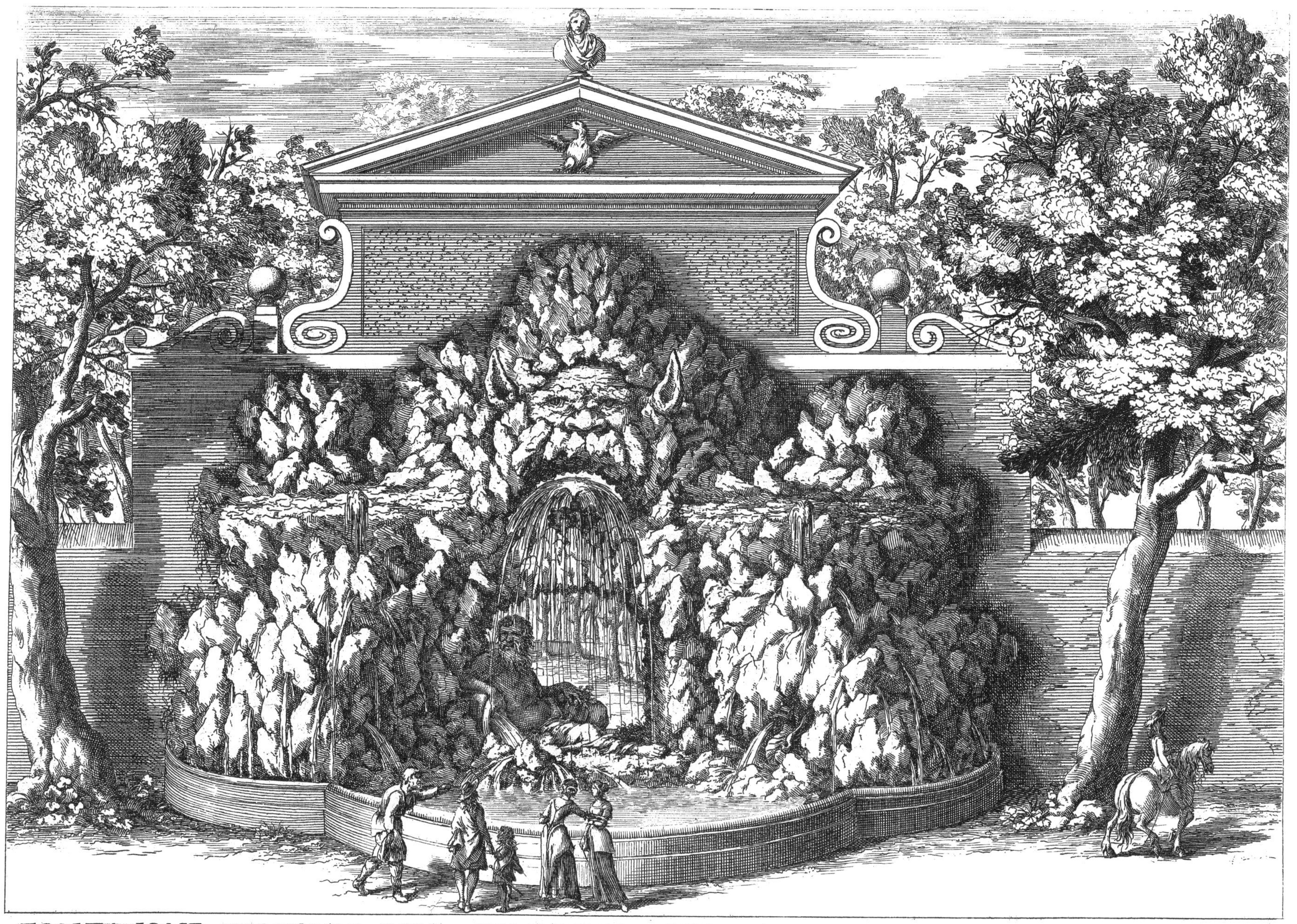

RUSTIC FOUNTAIN IN THE GARDEN OF PRINCE BORGHESE OUTSIDE PORTA PINCIANA, KNOWN AS FOUNTAIN OF THE MASK, FACING THE GATE AT THE ENTRANCE TO VIALE DEGLI OLMI. ARCHITECTURE BY GIO. ANTONIO VANSANTIO.

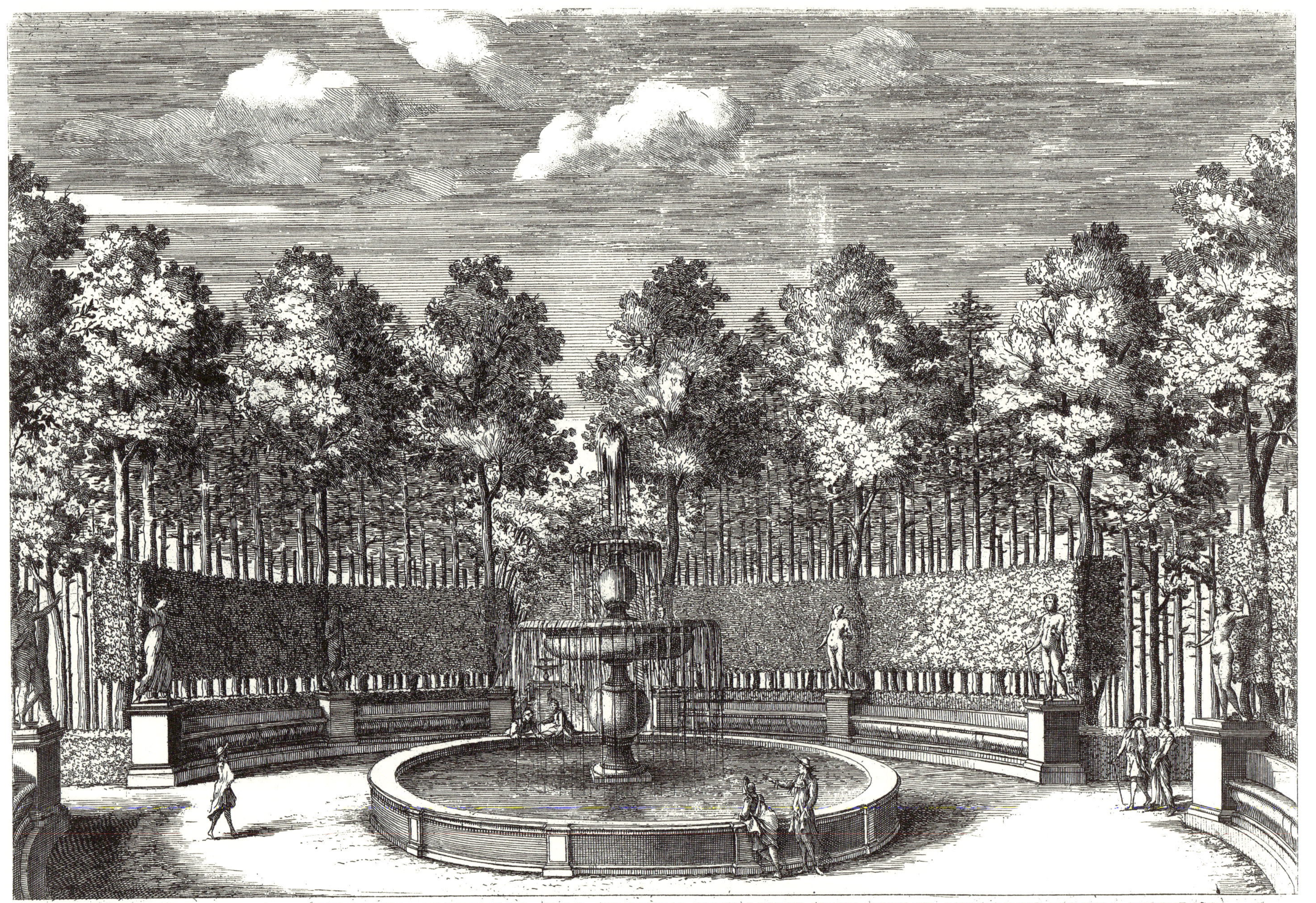

TWO SIMILAR FOUNTAINS WITH TWIN MARBLE BOWLS IN THE GARDEN OF PRINCE BORGHESE OUTSIDE PORTA PINCIANA, LOCATED UNDER THE PALACE AMONG FENCES AND WISTERIA-LINED BOULEVARDS ADORNED WITH STATUES. ARCHITECTURE BY GIO. ANTONIO VANSANTIO.

56

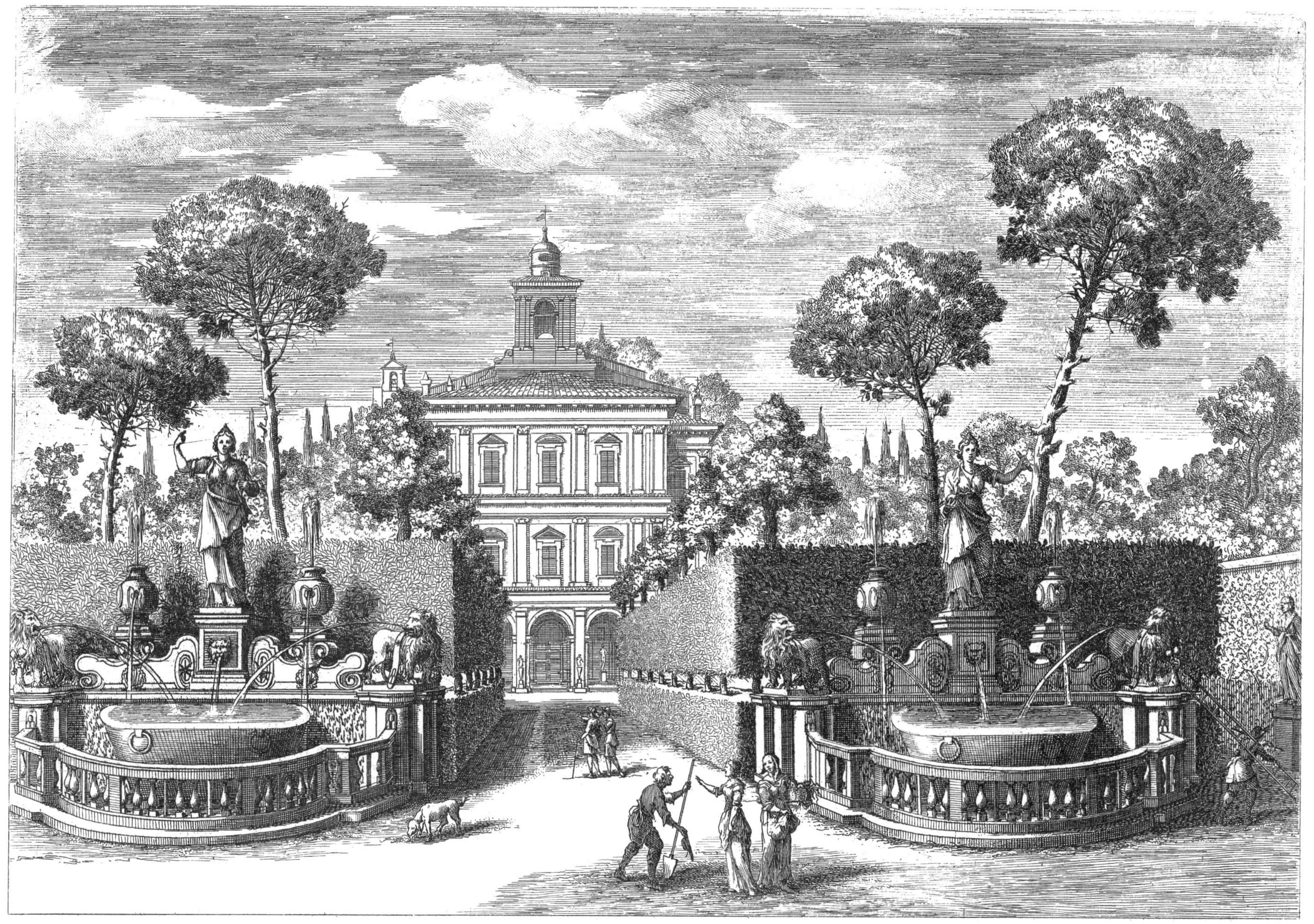

FONTANA NEL GIARDINO MONTALTO

su l monte Viminale uerso Santa Maria maggiore. Architettura del Caualier Domenico Fontana

FOUNTAIN IN THE MONTALTO GARDEN ON THE VIMINAL HILL TOWARDS ST. MARY MAJOR. ARCHITECTURE BY SIR DOMENICO FONTANA.

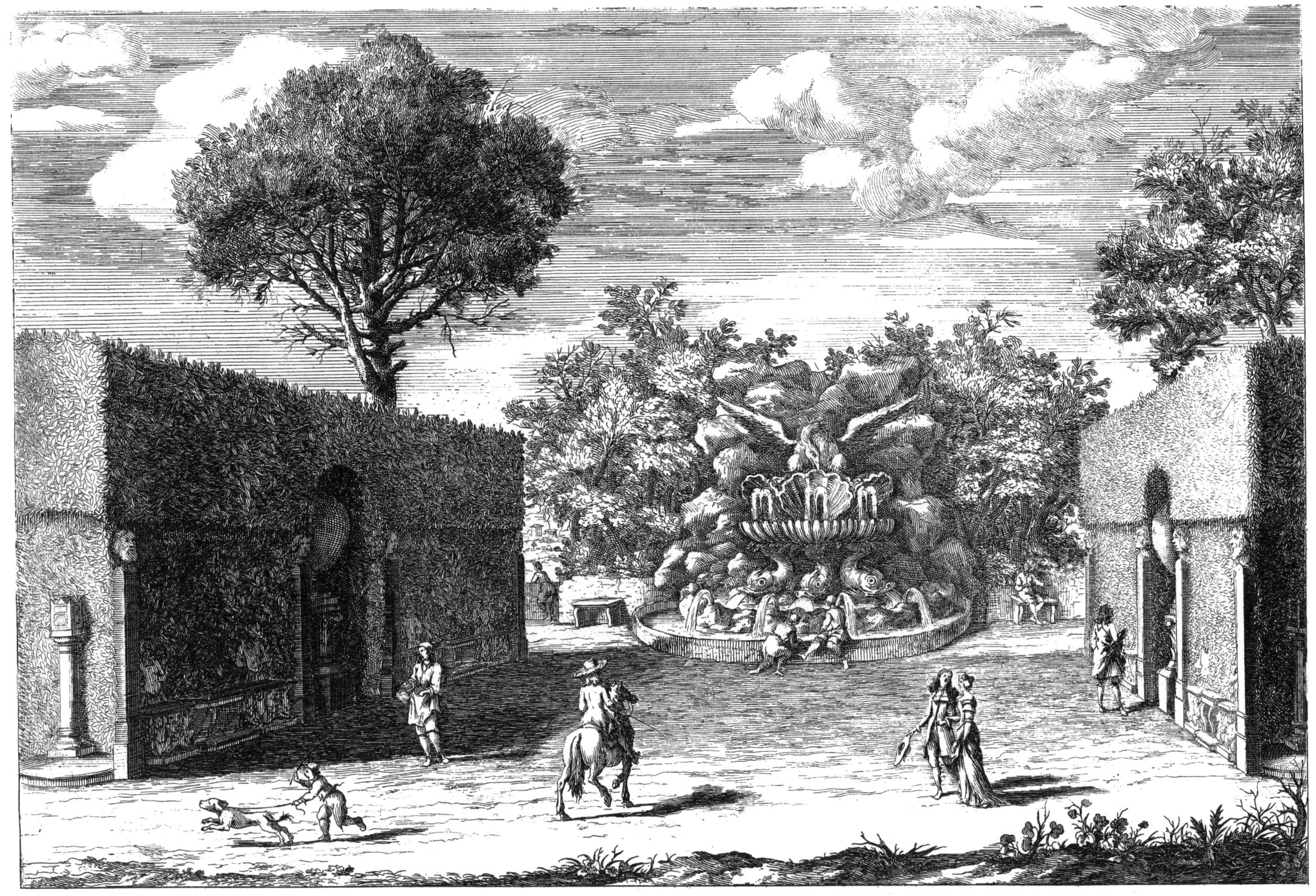

FONTAIN OF THE EAGLE IN THE GARDEN OF DUKE MATTEI IN PIAZZA DELLA NAVICELLA.
ARCHITECTURE BY SIR GIO. LORENZO BERNINI.

58

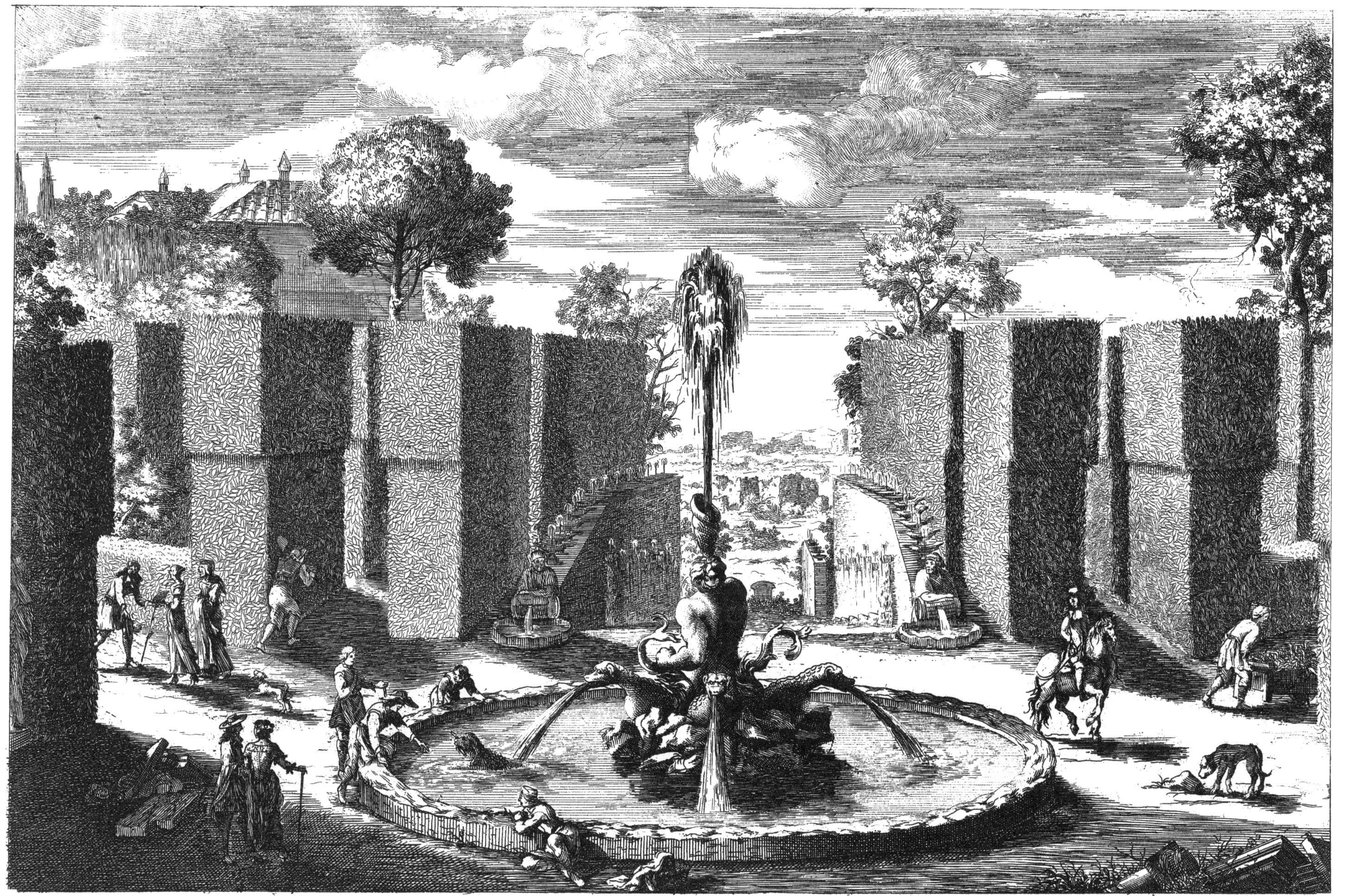

FONTANA DEL TRITONE A CAPO IL VIALE DELLE FONTANELLE NEL GIARDINO

del Signor Duca Máttei alla Nauicella. Architettura del Caualier Gio. Lorenzo Bernini.

FOUNTAIN OF TRITON AT THE ENTRANCE TO VIALE DELLE FONTANELLE, IN THE GARDEN OF DUKE MATTEI IN PIAZZA DELLA NAVICELLA.
ARCHITECTURE BY SIR GIO. LORENZO BERNINI.

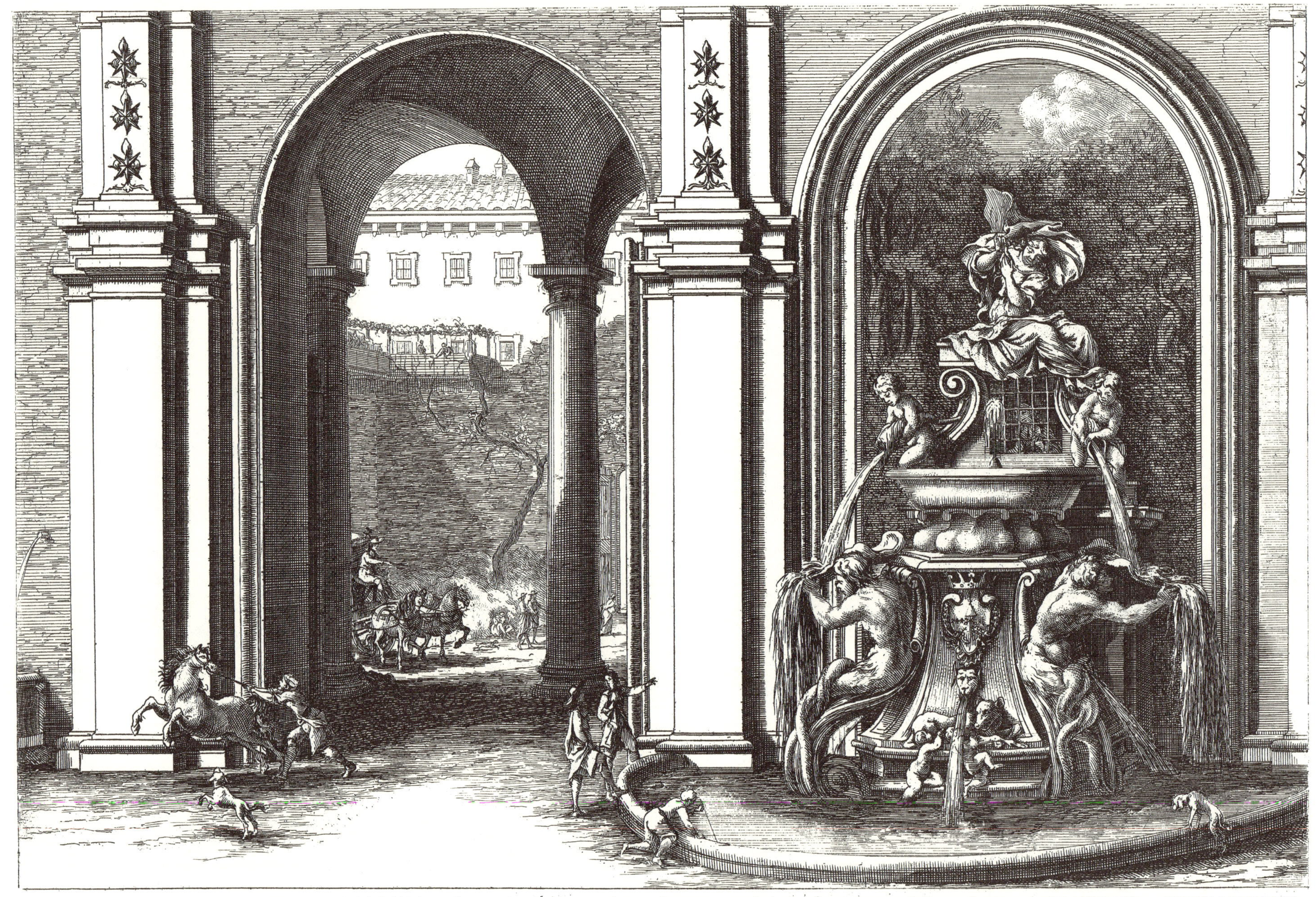

FONTANA SITVATA NEL CORTILE GRANDE DEL PALAZZO NVOVO DEL SIGNOR PRENCIPE
Panfilio nella Piazza del Colleggio Romano. Architettura del Caualiere Alessandro Algardi.
FOUNTAIN IN THE LARGE COURTYARD OF THE NEW PALACE OF PRINCE PAMPHILI IN PIAZZA DEL COLLEGIO ROMANO.
ARCHITECTURE BY SIR ALESSANDRO ALGARDI.

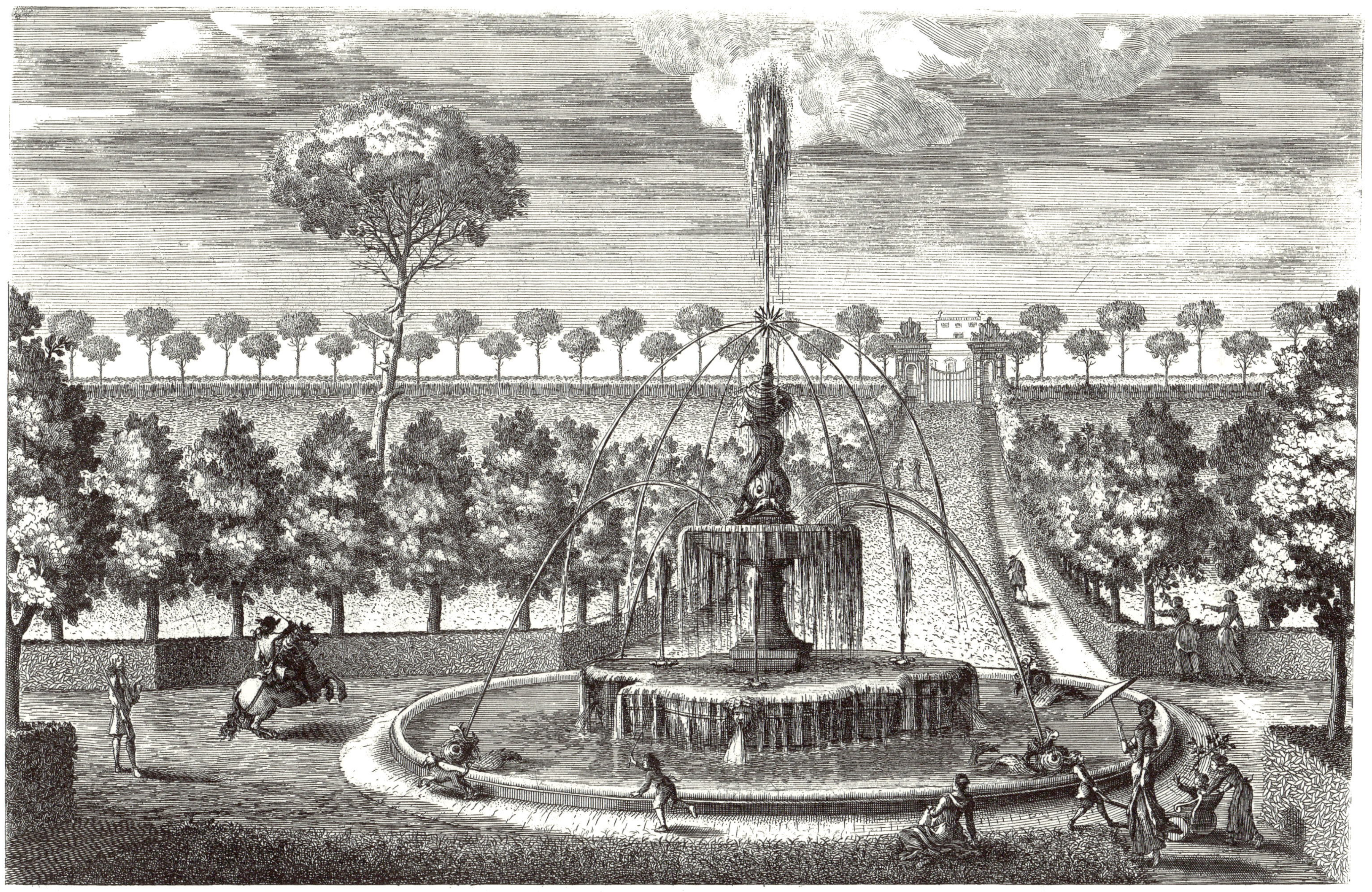

FONTANA DETTA DELLA REGINA NEL GIARDINO DEL SIGNOR PRINCIPE PAMPHILIO À SAN PANCRATIO.
Architettura del Caualier Alessandro Algardi.

FOUNTAIN KNOWN AS FOUNTAIN OF THE QUEEN IN THE GARDEN OF PRINCE PAMPHILI IN SAN PANCRAZIO.
ARCHITECTURE BY SIR ALESSANDRO ALGARDI.

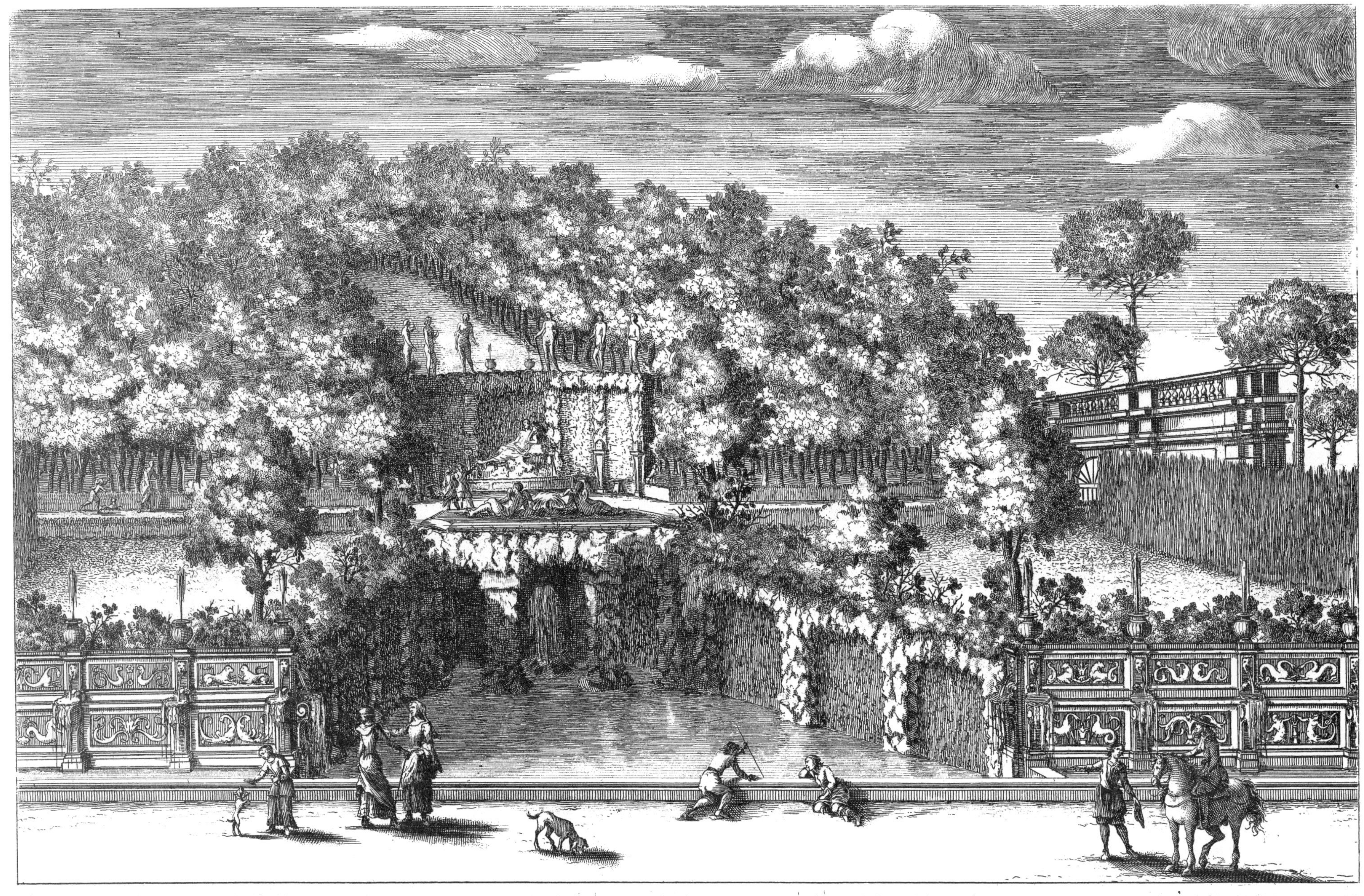

VIEW OF THE FOUNTAINS ON THE RIGHT SIDE OF THE THEATER IN THE GARDEN OF PRINCE PAMPHILI IN SAN PANCRAZIO.
ARCHITECTURE BY SIR ALESSANDRO ALGARDI.

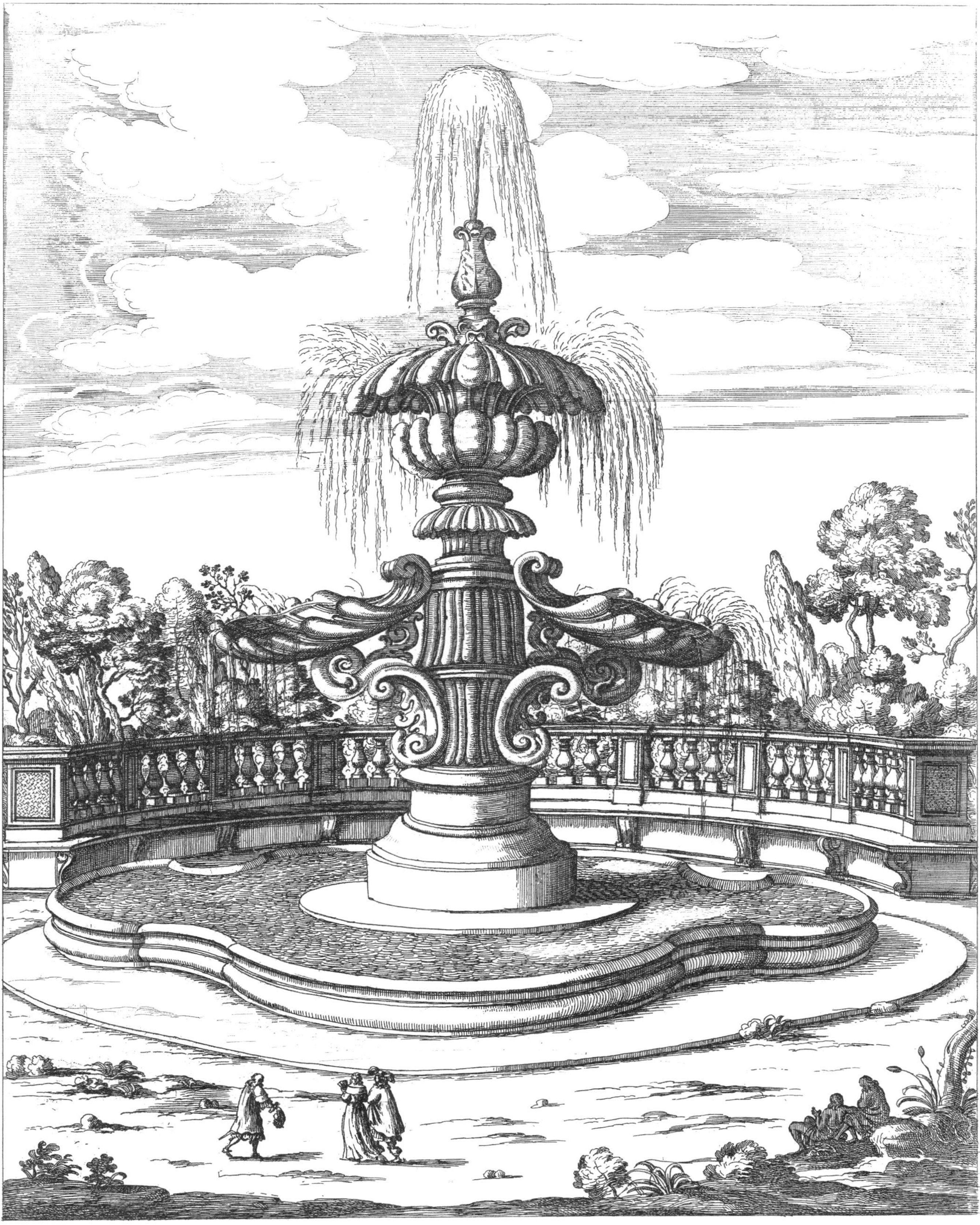

LILII PAMPHYLII FONS

The Fountain of Lilius Pamphylius

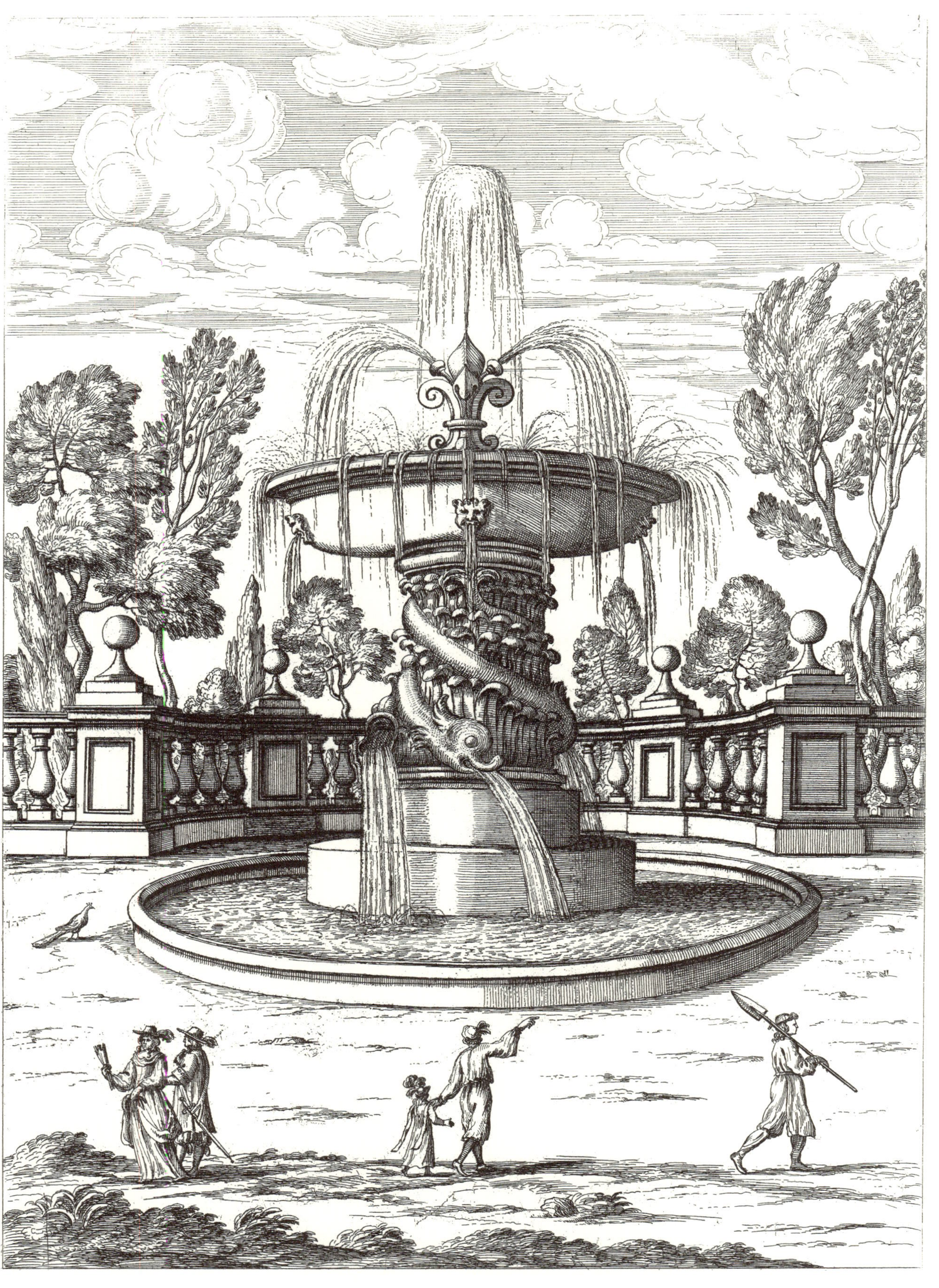

FONS E CONSPECTV PRINCIPIS PORTAE VILLAE PAMPHYLIAE.

THE FOUNTAIN SEEN FROM THE VIEW OF THE MAIN GATE OF THE VILLA OF PAMPHILIA.

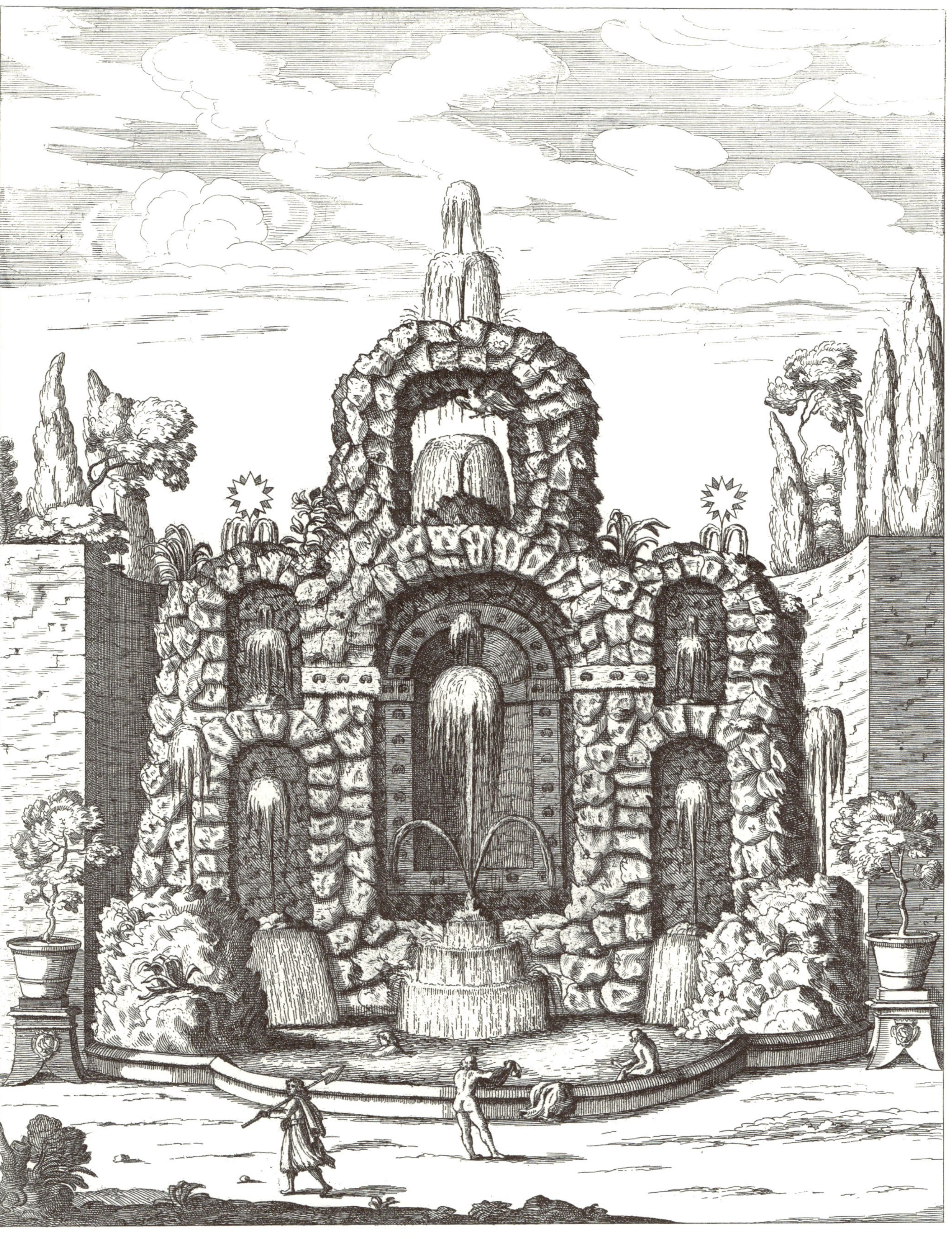

COLVMBAE PAMPHYLIAE FONS.

Columba Pamphilia Fountain

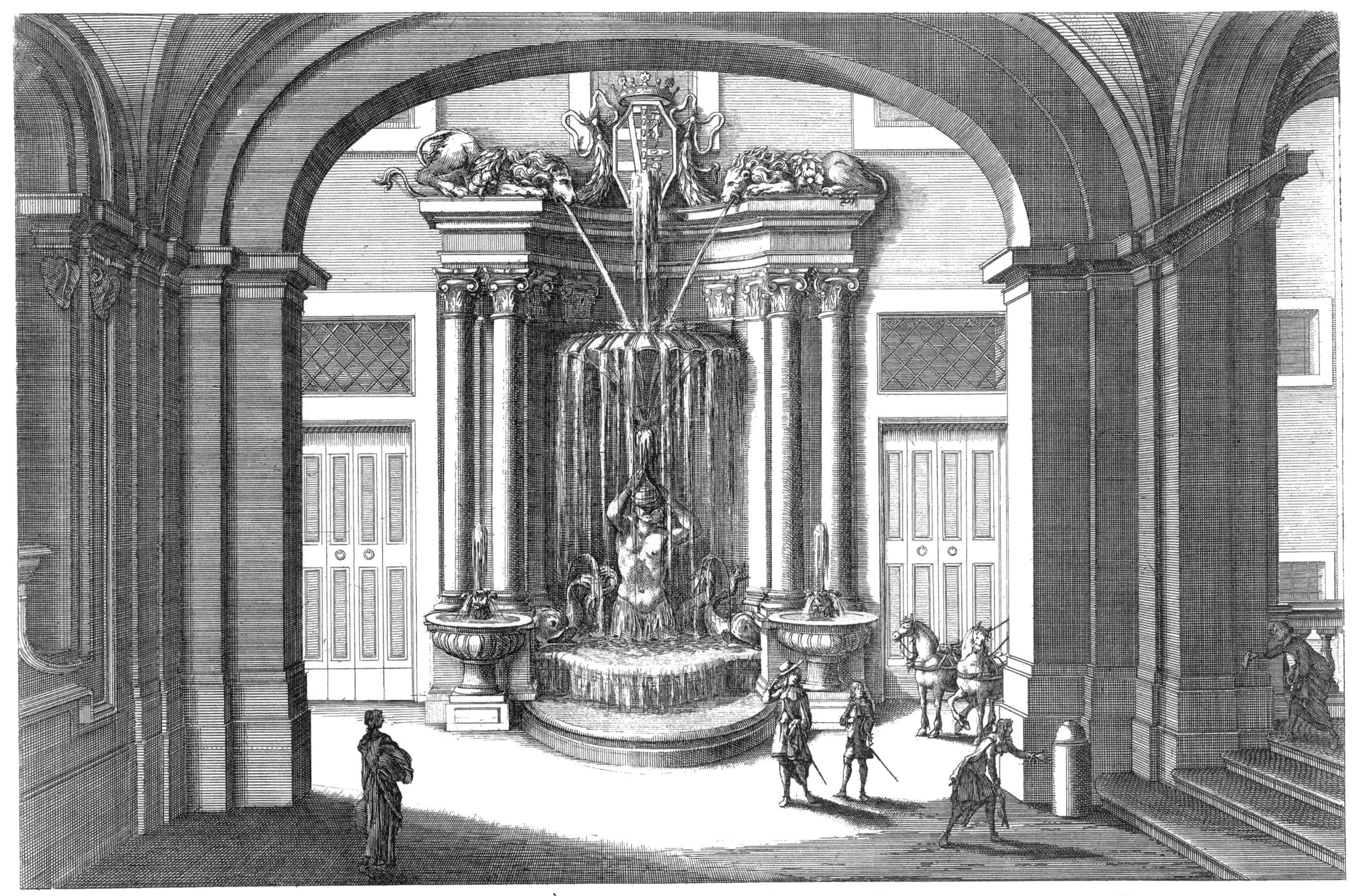

FOUNTAIN IN PALAZZO MASSIMI UNDER THE CAPITOLINE HILL. ARCHITECTURE BY SIR CARLO FONTANA.

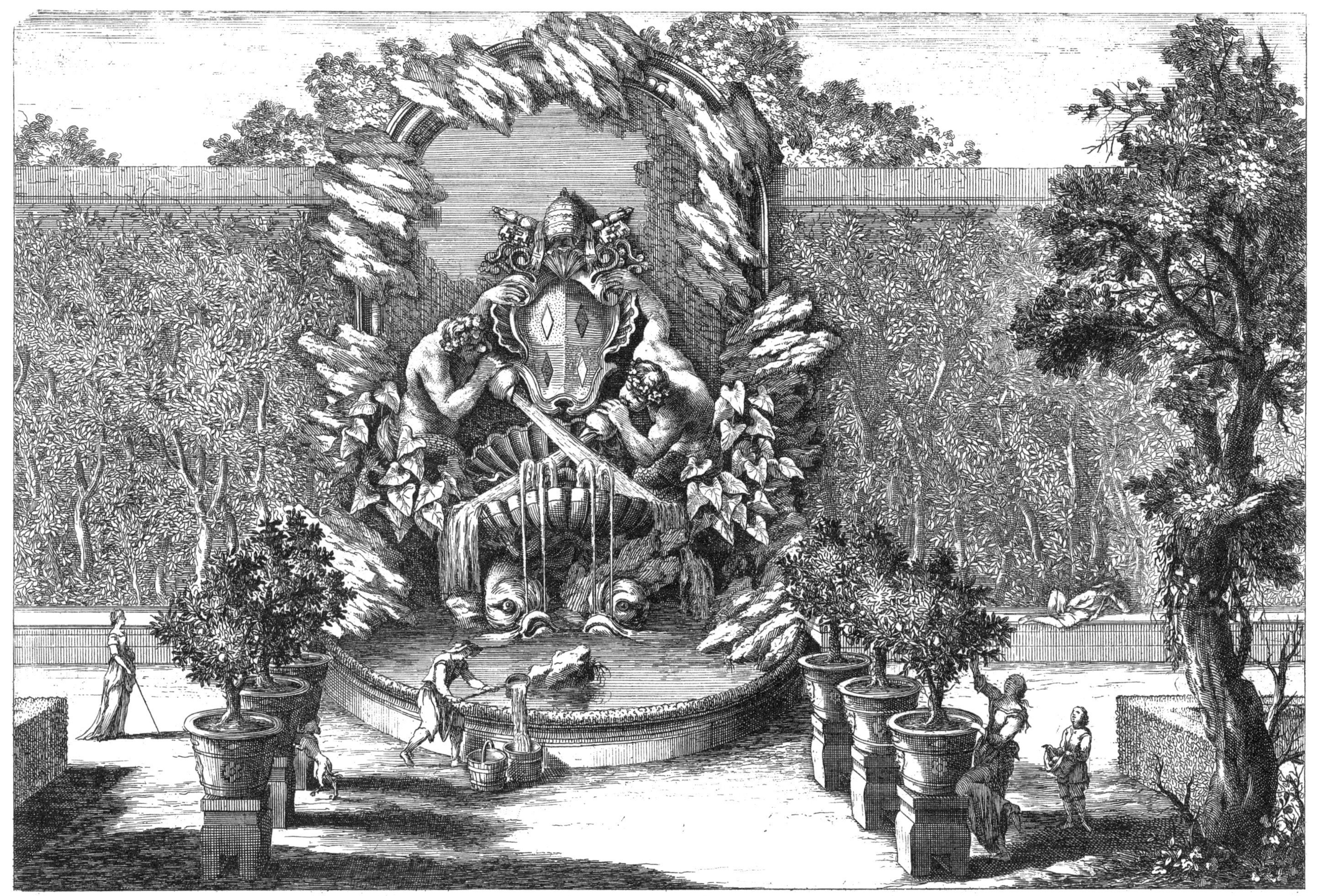

FONTANA NELLA CASA DEL SIGNOR PAOLO STRADA SITVATA IN STRADA NOVA.

Architettura del Caualier Gio. Lorenzo Bernini.

FOUNTAIN IN THE HOUSE OF SIR PAOLO STRADA, LOCATED IN STRADA NUOVA. ARCHITECTURE BY SIR GIO. LORENZO BERNINI.

LE FONTANE
DEL GIARDINO ESTENSE
IN TIVOLI
CON LI LORO PROSPETTI, E VEDVTE DELLA CASCATA
DEL FIVME ANIENE

DISEGNATE, ET INTAGLIATE
DA GIO: FRANCESCO VENTVRINI

PARTE QVARTA

Data in luce da Gio: Giacomo de Rossi nella sua stamperia,

in Roma alla Pace, all' Insegna di Parigi con Priu. del S. Pont.

FOUNTAINS IN THE GARDEN OF THE VILLA D'ESTE IN TIVOLI WITH THEIR FRONTAL VIEWS, AND VIEWS OF THE ANIENE RIVER WATERFALL. DRAWN AND ENGRAVED BY GIO. FRANCESCO VENTURINI. PART FOUR. PRINTED BY GIO. GIACOMO DE ROSSI FOR HIS PRESS IN VIA DELLA PACE IN ROME, BY THE PARIGI SIGN, AND WITH THE PATRONAGE OF THE HOLY FATHER.

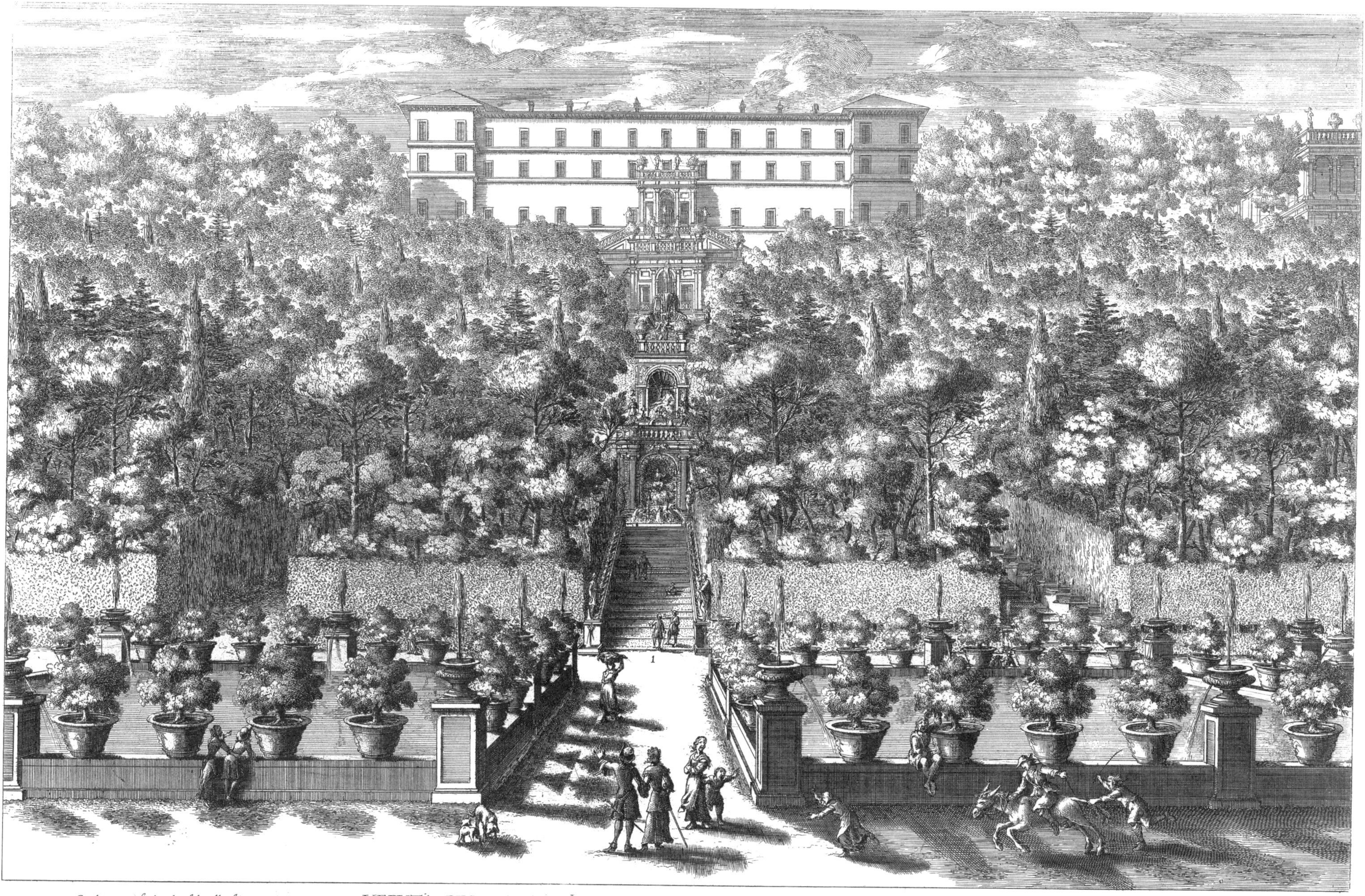

PANORAMIC VIEW OF THE VILLA FROM THE GARDEN AND ITS FOUNTAINS.

1. SLOPE AND STAIRS LEADING TO THE FOUNTAIN OF DRAGONS
2. VIALONE DELLE FONTANELLE

3. FOUNTAIN OF THE GREAT CUP
4. FOUNTAIN OF THE HYDRA

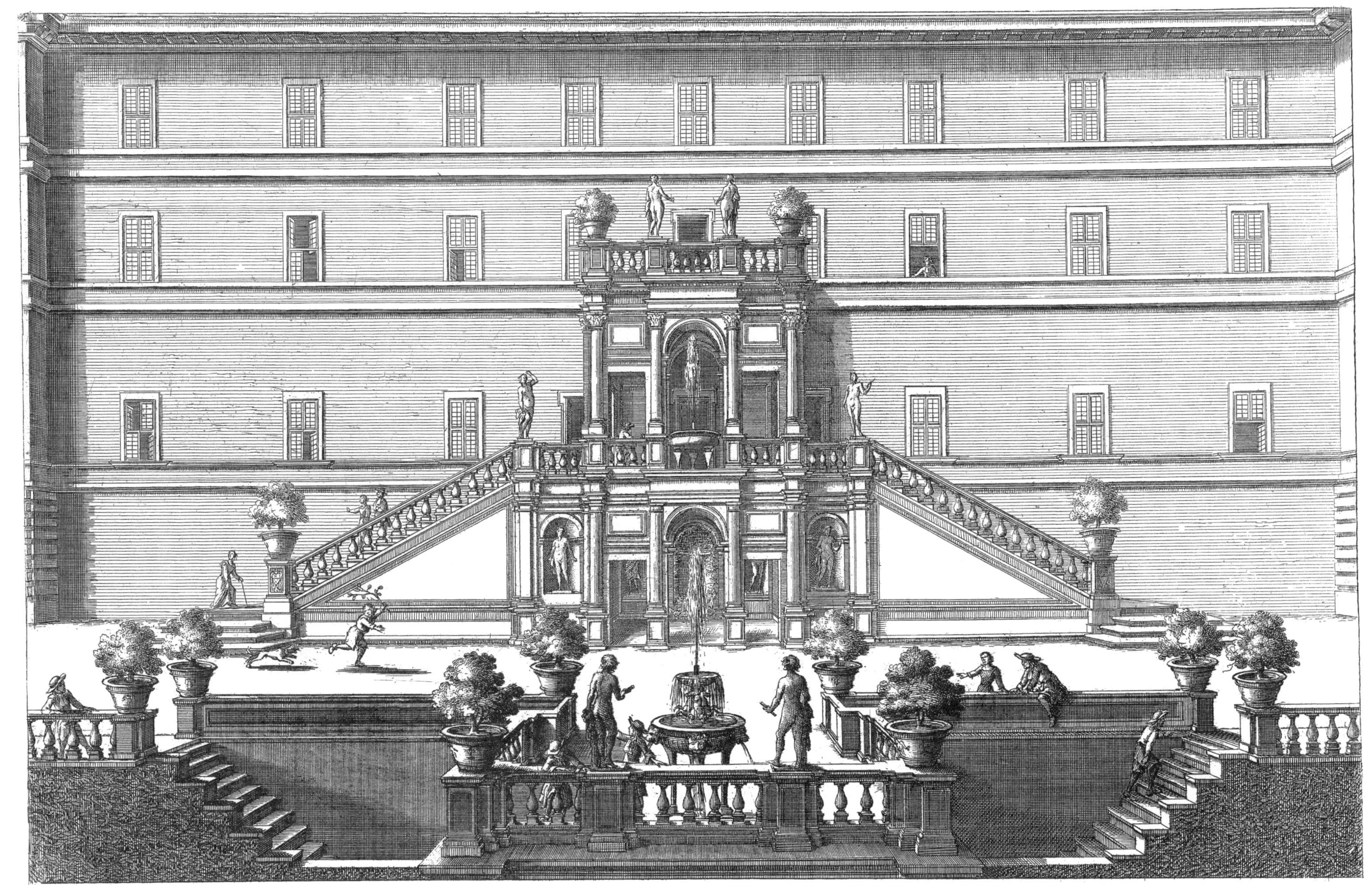

VEDVTA E PROSPETTO DEL PALAZZO NEL GIARDINO

VIEW AND FAÇADE OF THE VILLA IN THE GARDEN.

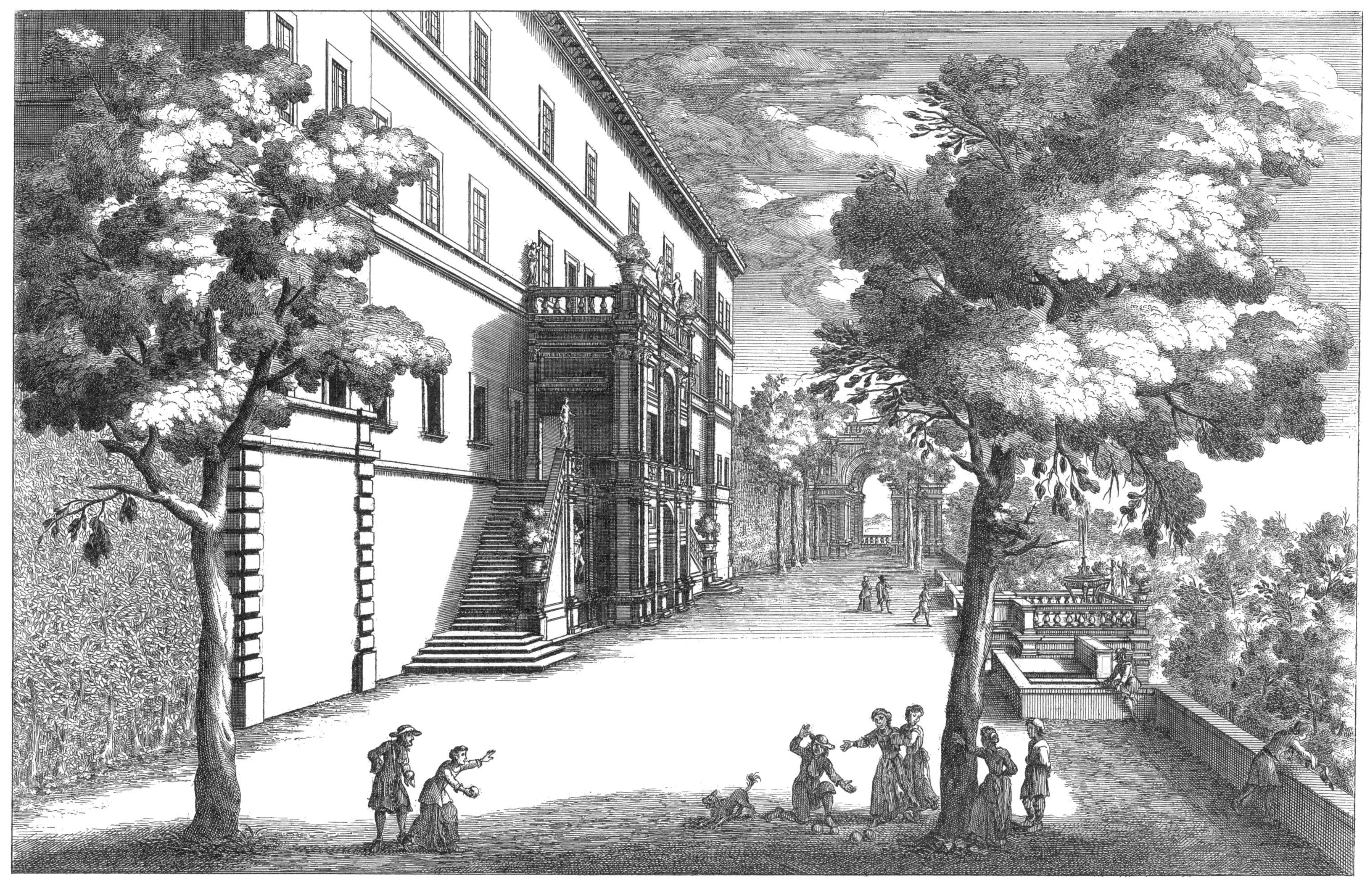

Side view of the villa in the garden of the Villa d'Este in Tivoli.

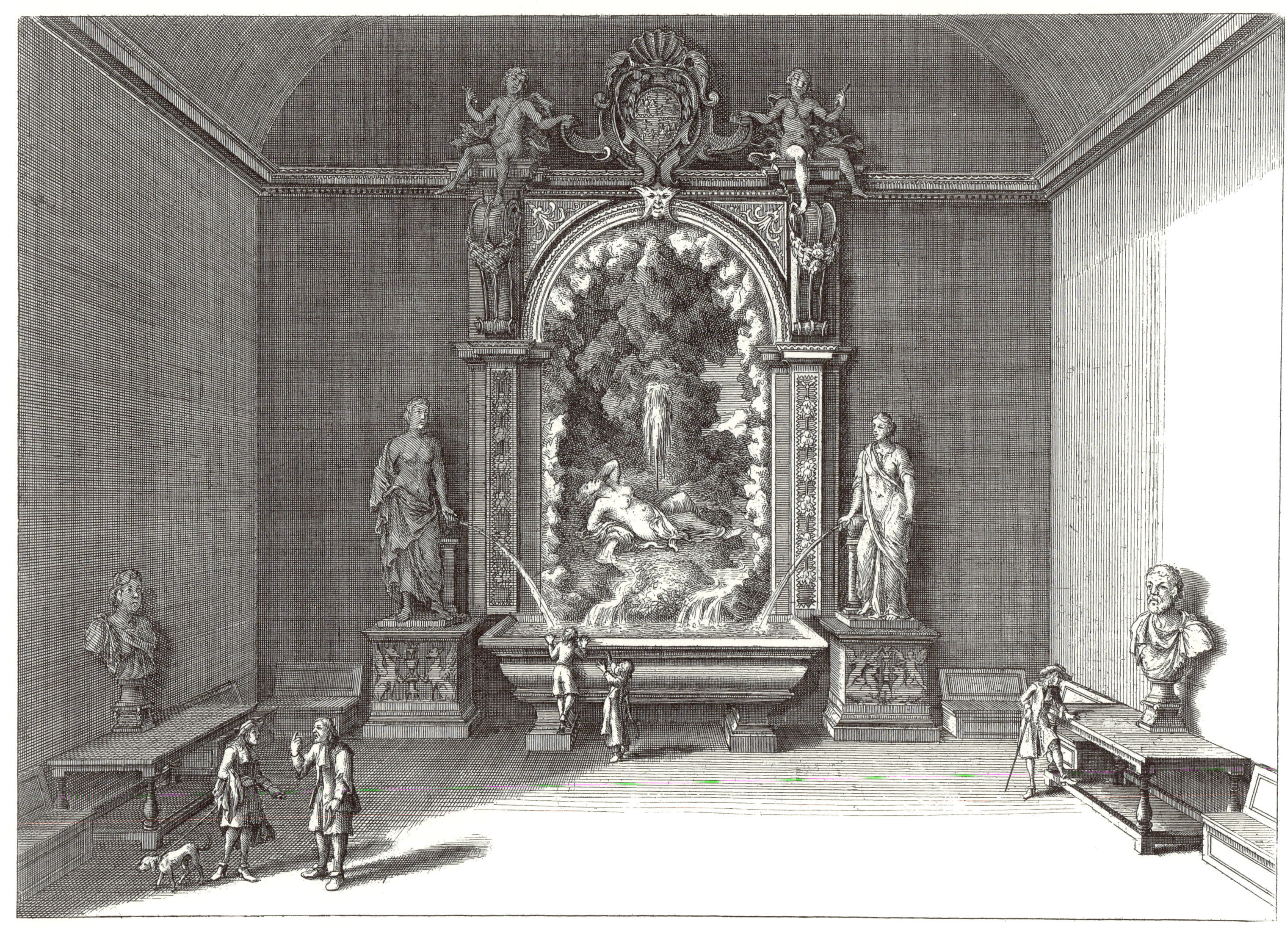

FOUNTAIN OF VENUS IN ONE OF THE OUTERMOST ROOMS OF THE VILLA.

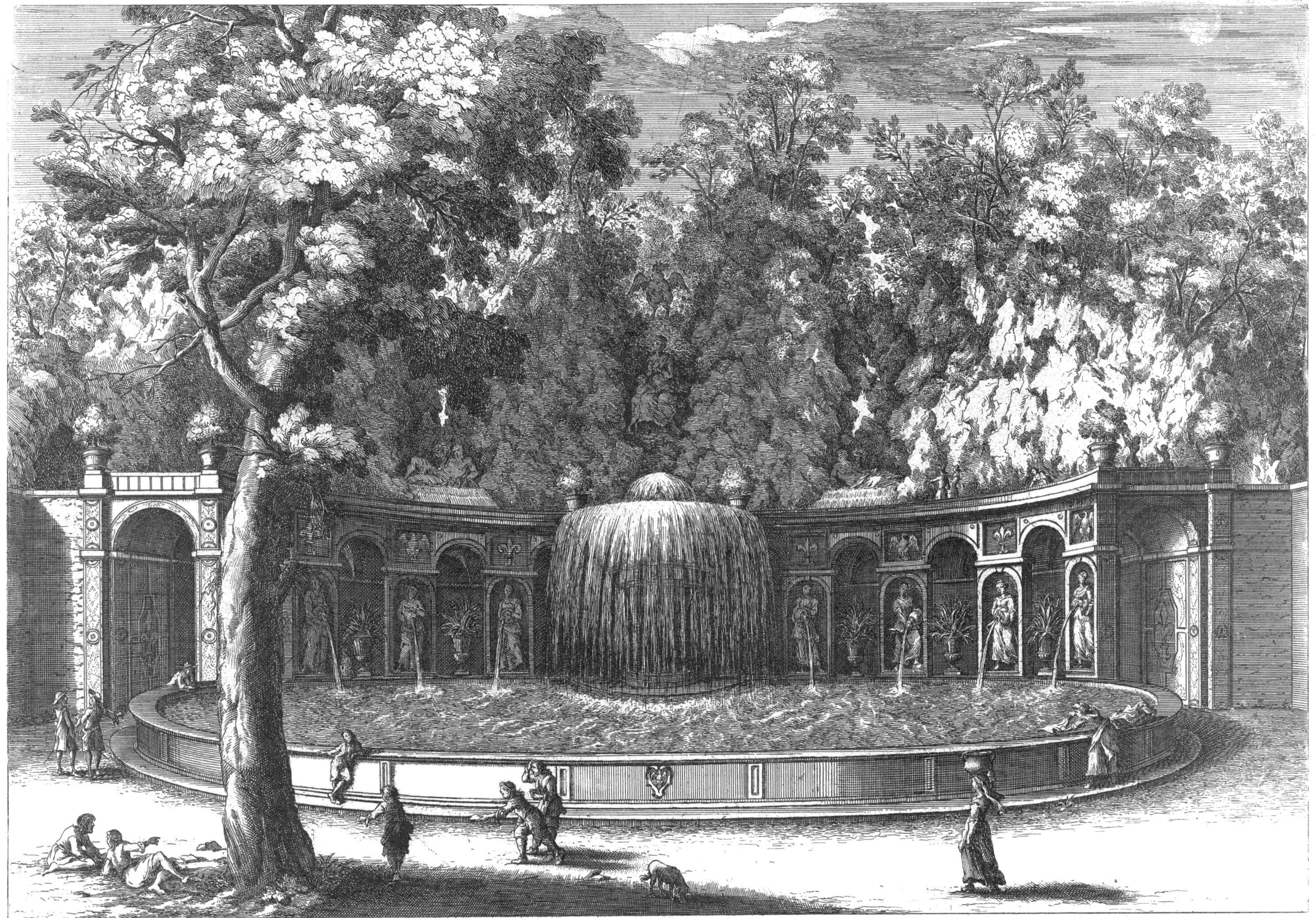

FOUNTAIN OF THE TIBURTINE SYBIL, OR ALBUNEA, KNOWN AS FONTANONE. WITH STATUES OF THE SYBIL AND OF THE RIVERS
ANIENE AND ERCULANEO, VIEWED FROM THE RIGHT SIDE OF THE VIALONE DELLE FONTANELLE.

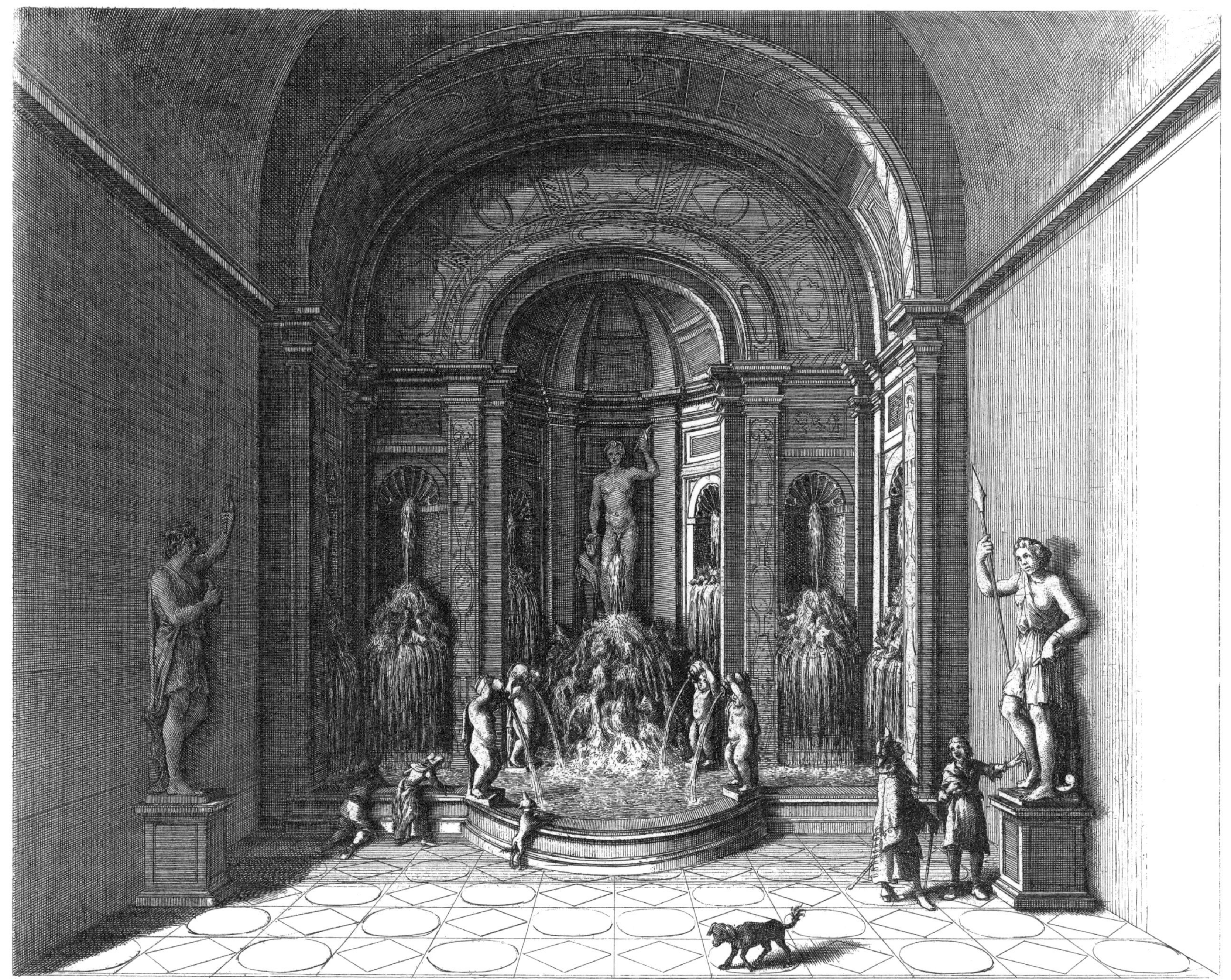

FOUNTAIN OF BACCHUS IN A ROOM ADJOINING THE FONTANONE ON THE SAME LEVEL OF THE VIALONE DELLE FONTANELLE.

74

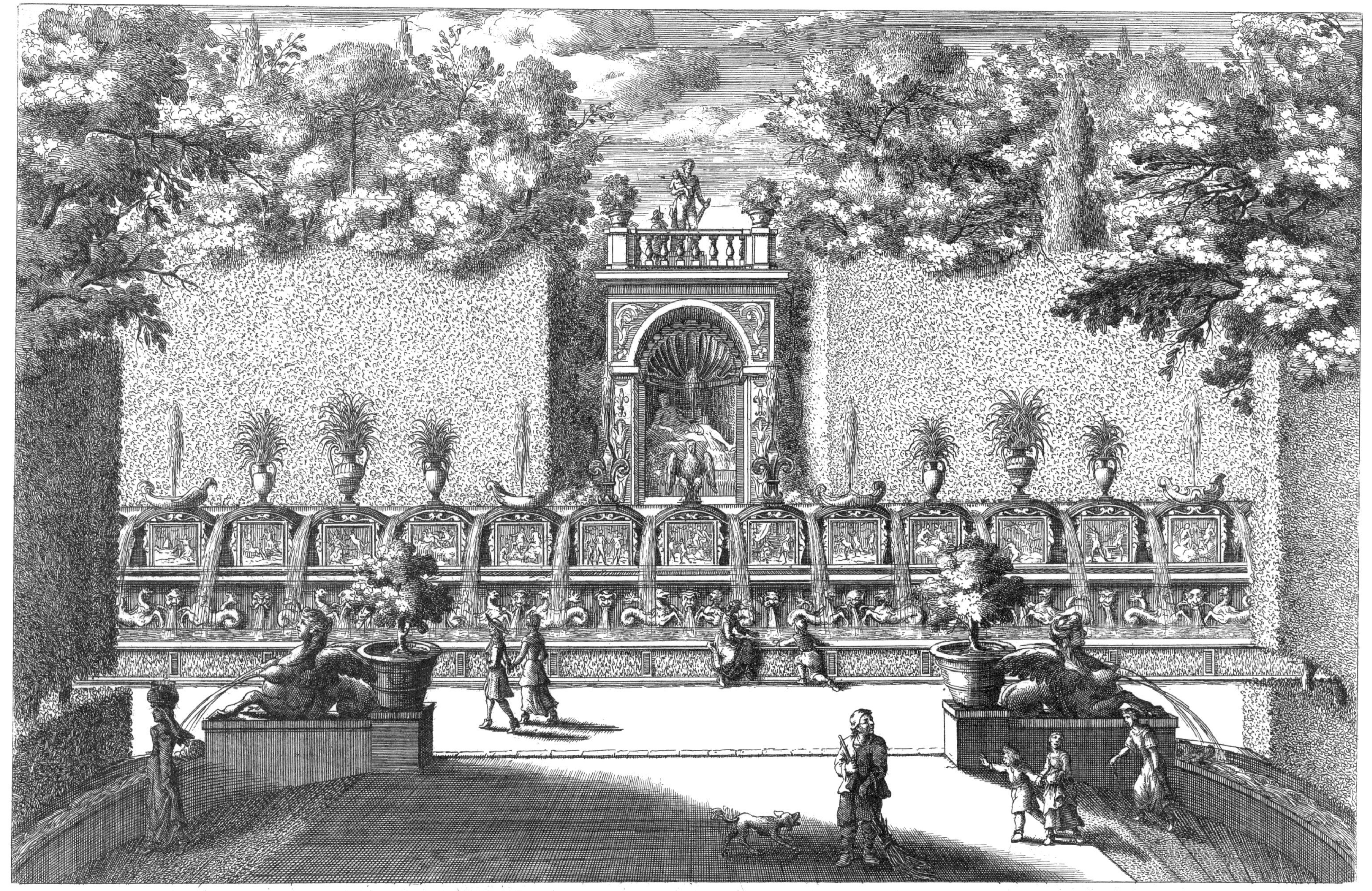

VEDVTA D' VNA PARTE DELLE FONTANELLE NEL VIALONE SOPRA LA FONTANA DE DRAGHI

Partial view of the Fontanelle on the boulevard above the Fountain of the Dragons.

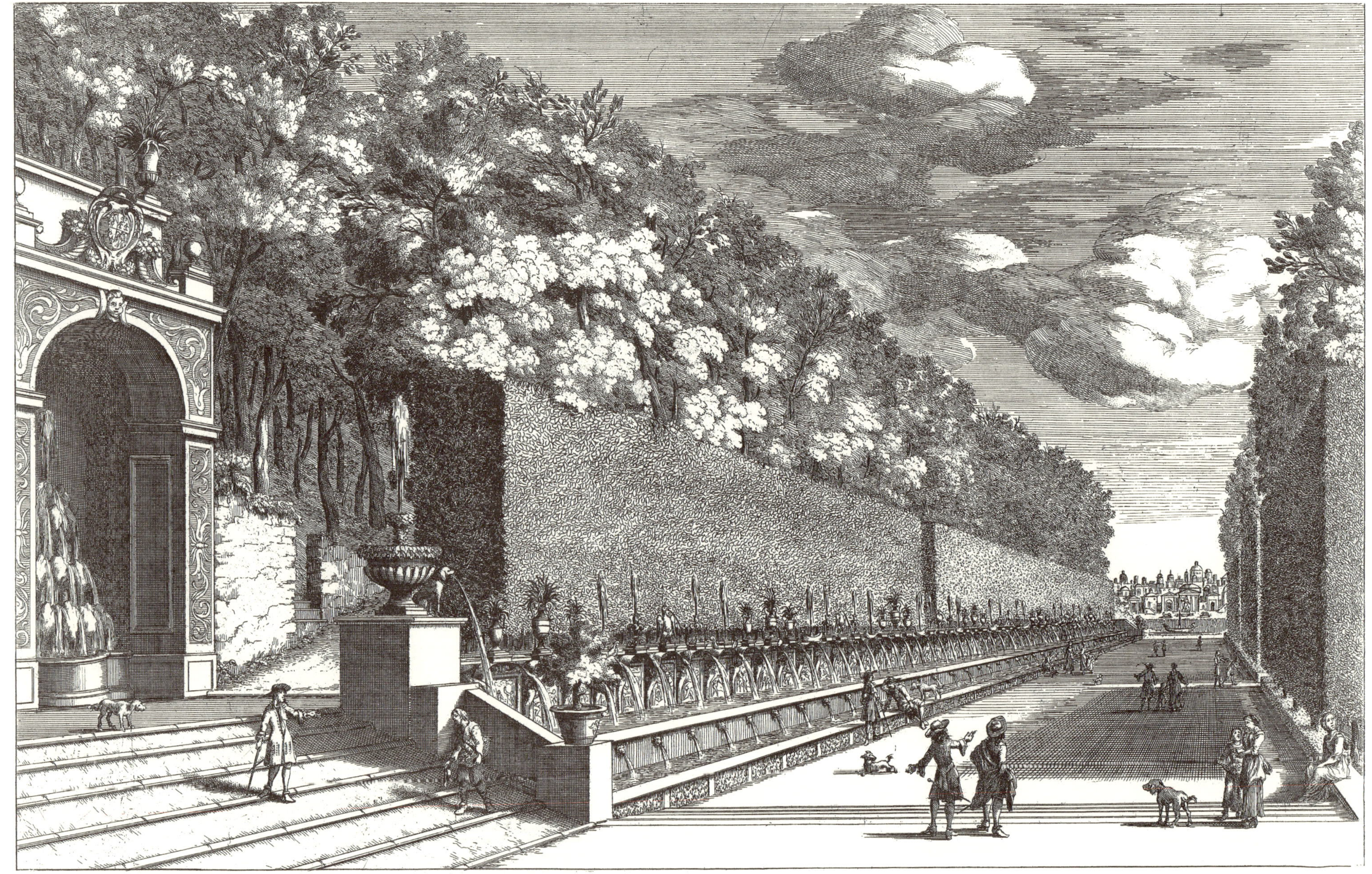

ALTRA VEDVTA PRINCIPALE IN PROFILO DEL VIALONE GRANDE DETTO DELLE FONTANELLE NEL GIARDINO ESTENSE IN TIVOLI

ALTERNATE SIDE VIEW OF THE GRAND BOULEVARD KNOWN AS VIALONE DELLE FONTANELLE IN THE GARDEN OF THE VILLA D'ESTE IN TIVOLI.

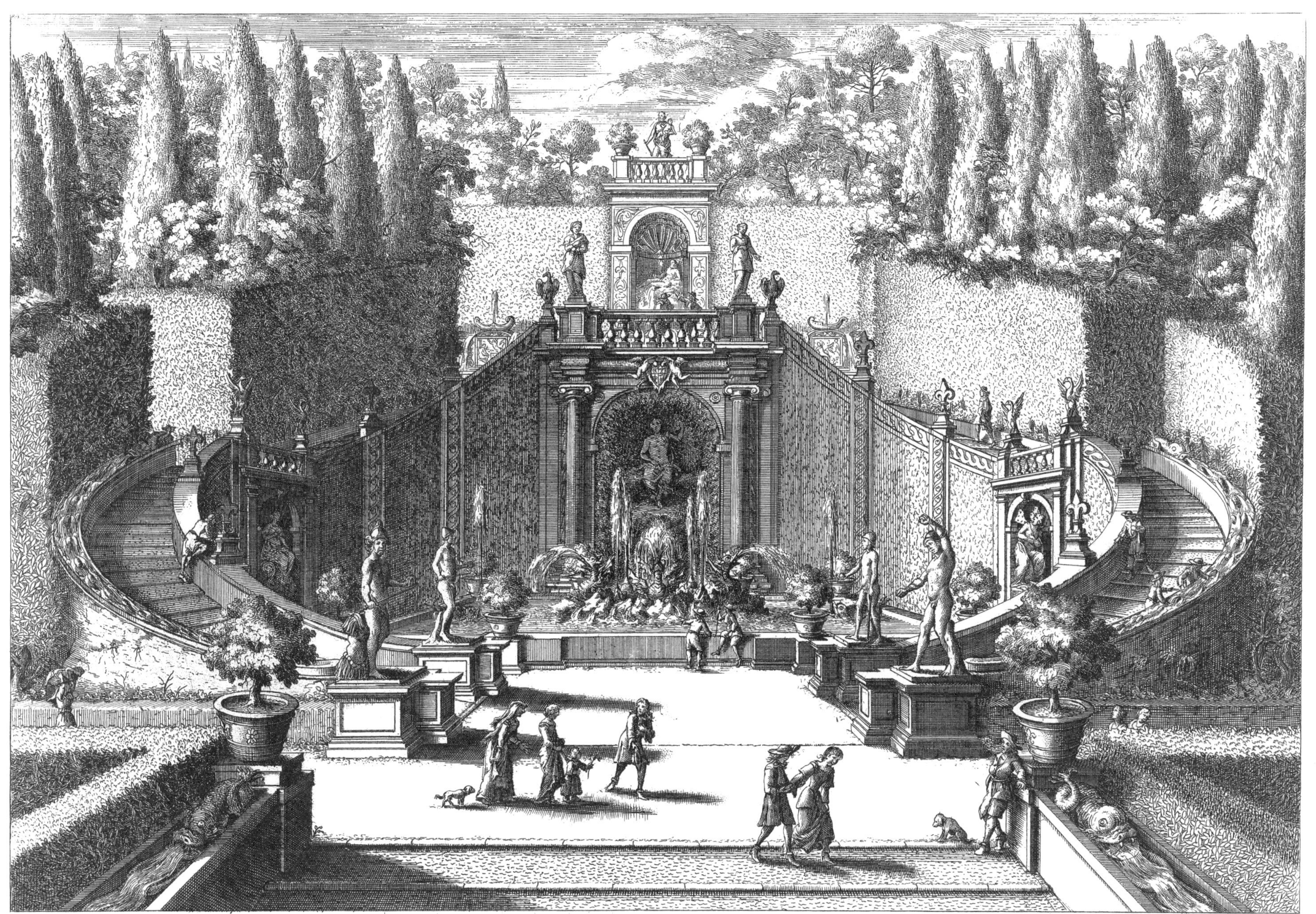

FOUNTAIN OF THE DRAGONS, KNOWN AS THE WINDMILL, BENEATH THE Vialone delle Fontanelle.

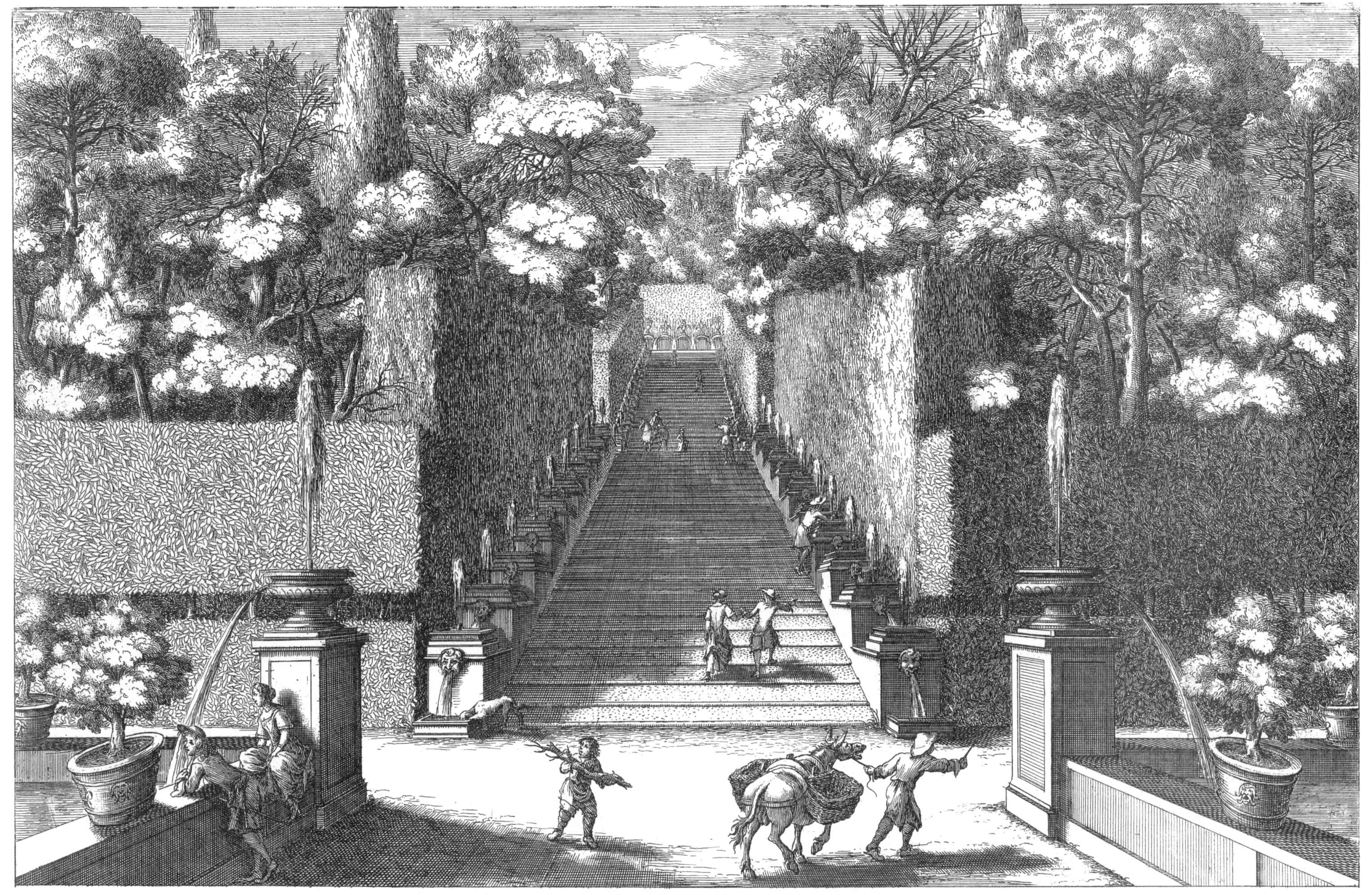

VIEW OF THE FOUNTAINS OF THE SLOPE AND STAIRS LEADING TO THE Vialone delle Fontanelle.

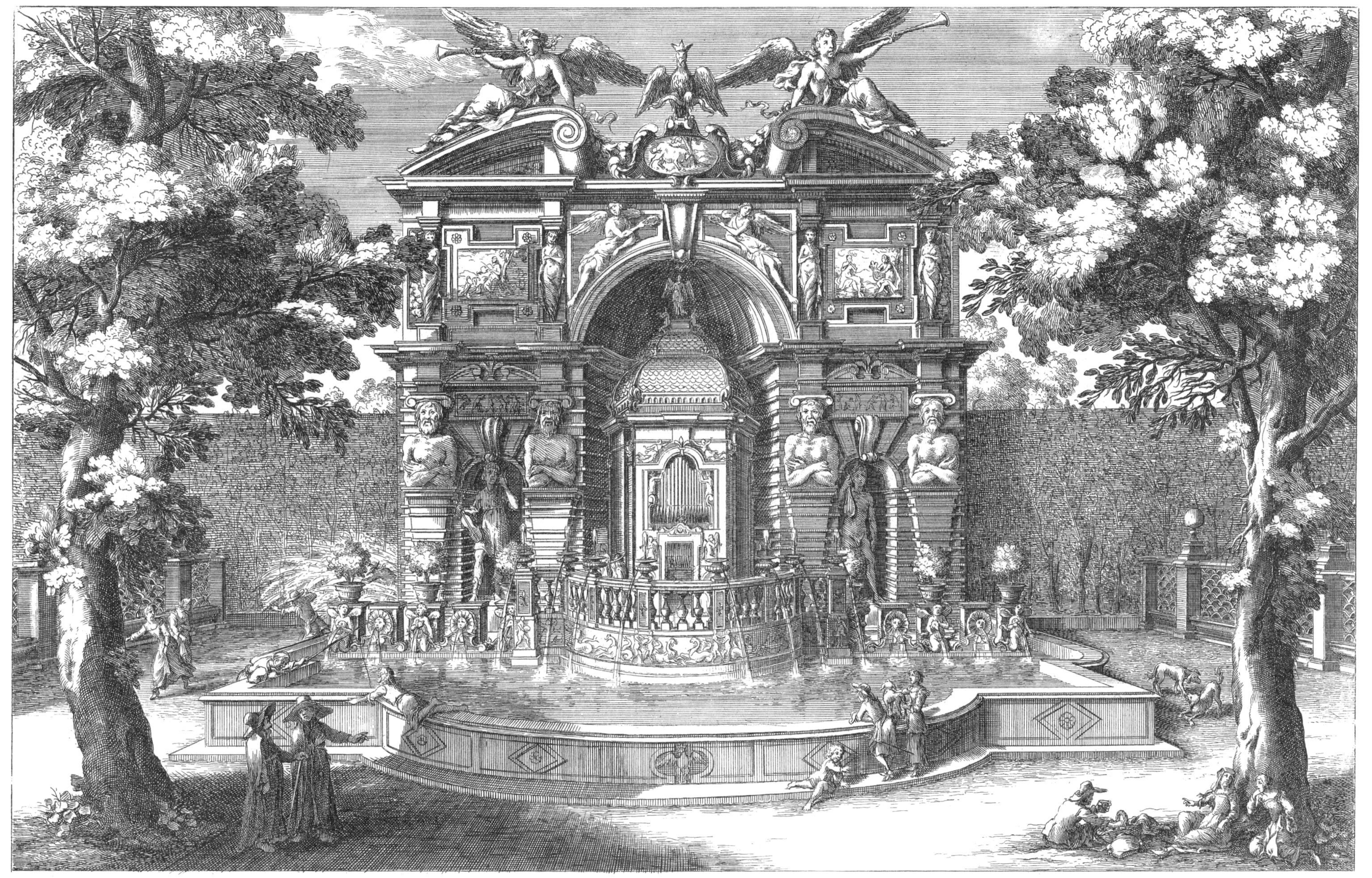

FONTANA DELL' ORGANO DAL LATO DESTRO NEL PIANO DEL VIALONE DELLE FONTANELLE

FOUNTAIN OF THE ORGAN ON THE RIGHT SIDE OF THE VIALONE DELLE FONTANELLE.

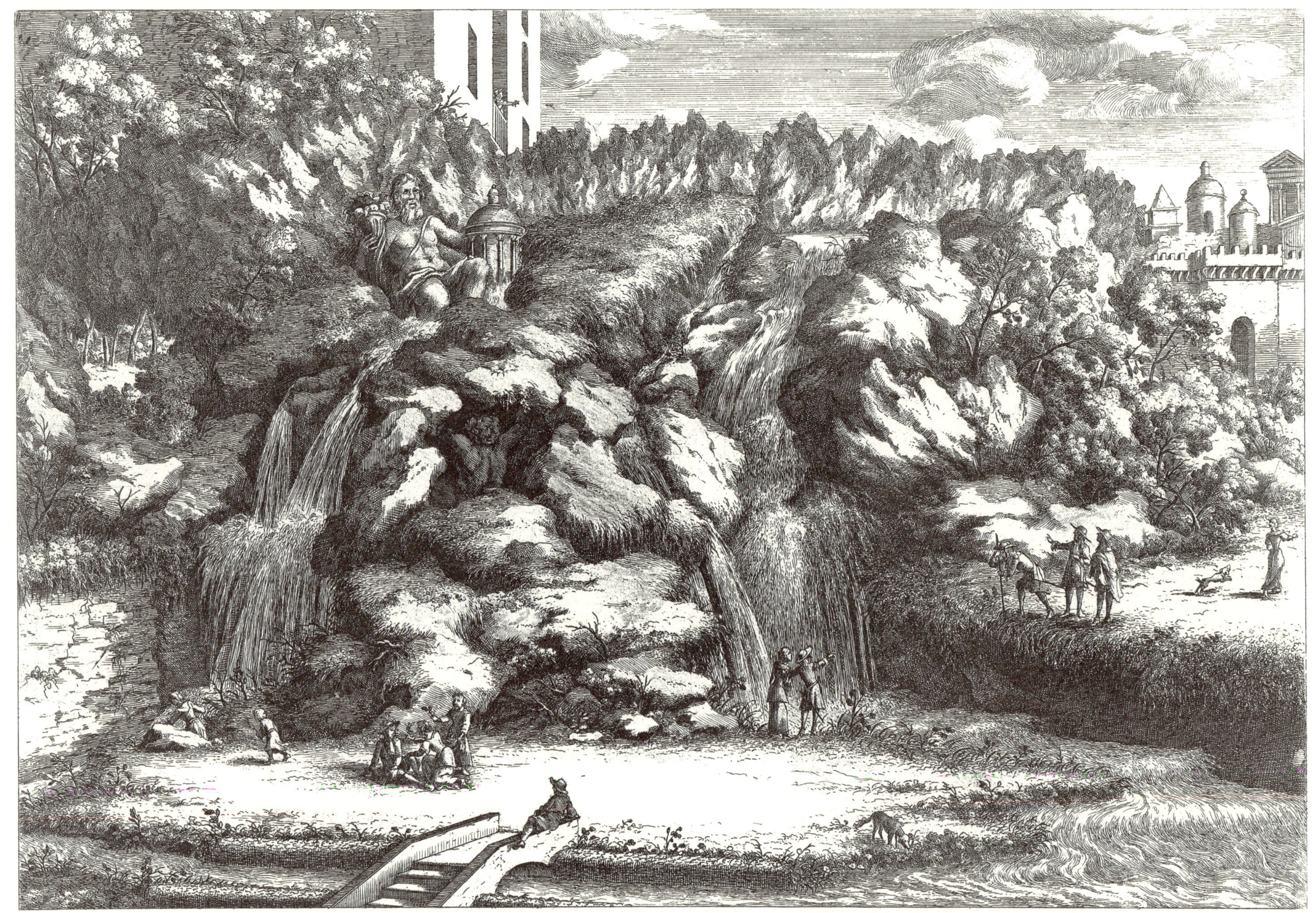

Frontal view and waterfall of the Aniene River with the Temple of the Sybil, next to the Fountain of Ancient Rome, on the level of the Vialone delle Fontanelle.

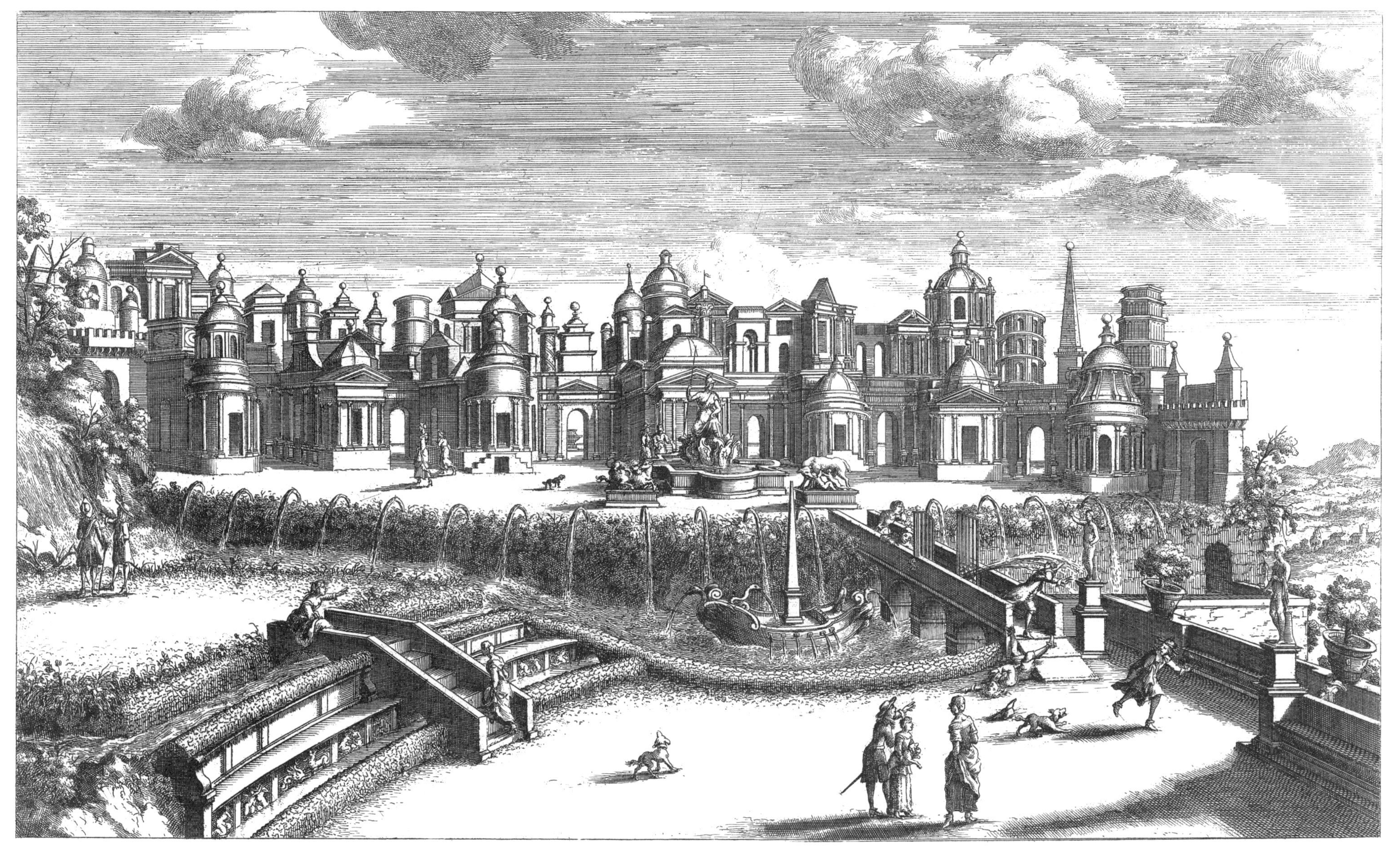

FONTANA, E PROSPETTO DI ROMA ANTICA CON L'ISOLA TIBERINA DAL LATO SINISTRO DEL VIALONE DELLE FONTANELLE

Frontal view of the Fountain of Ancient Rome, with Tiber Island, viewed from the left side of the Vialone delle Fontanelle.

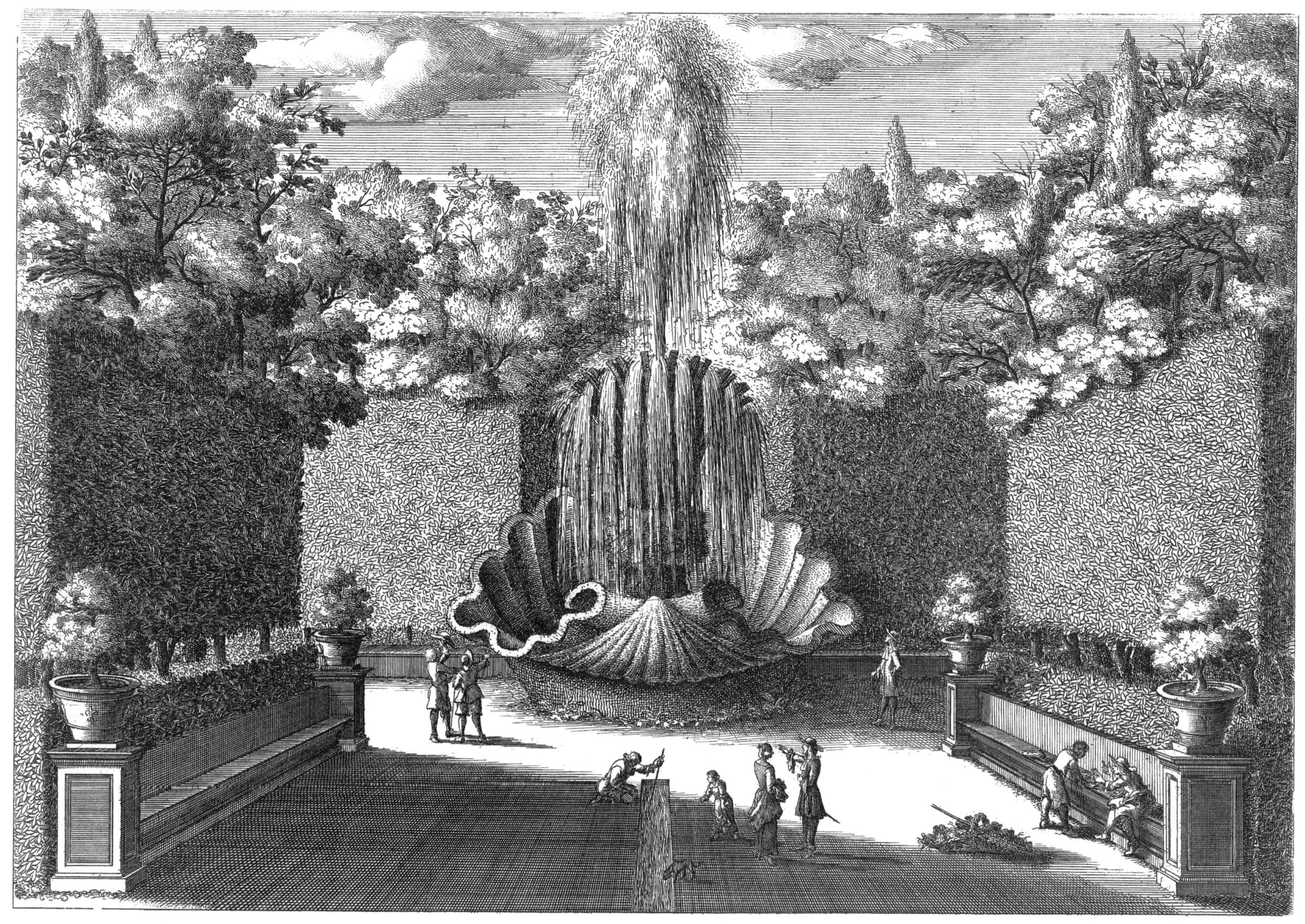

VEDVTA DELLA FONTANA DEL BICCHIERONE SOPRA IL VIALONE DELLE FONTANELLE
VIEW OF THE FOUNTAIN OF THE GREAT CUP, ABOVE THE VIALONE DELLE FONTANELLE.

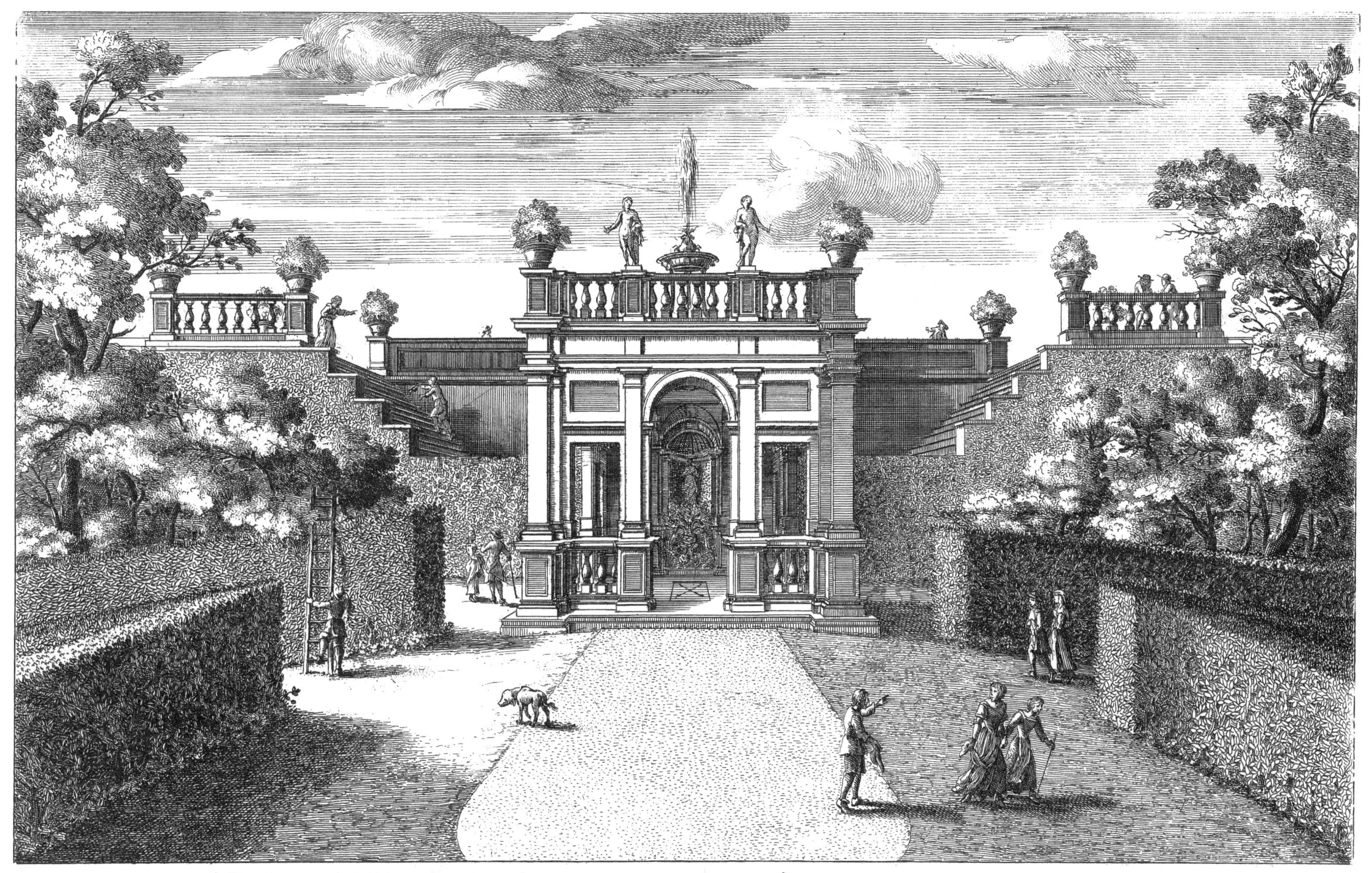

Fountain known as the Hydra located atop the Fountain of the Great Cup.

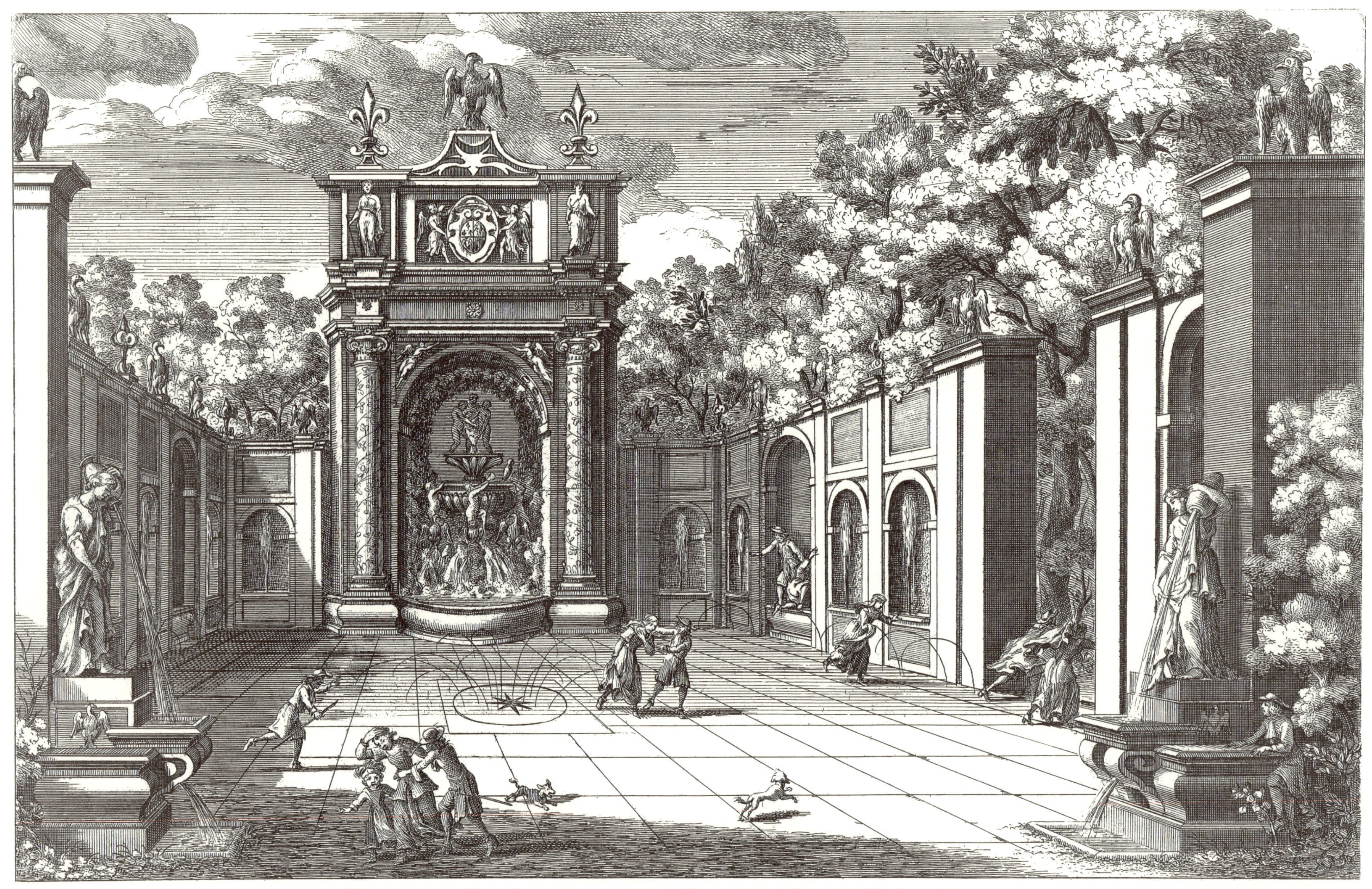

TEATRO, E FONTANA DELLA CIVETTA CON DIVERSI GIVOCHI D'ACQVA

THEATER AND FOUNTAIN OF THE OWL WITH VARIOUS WATERWORKS.

84

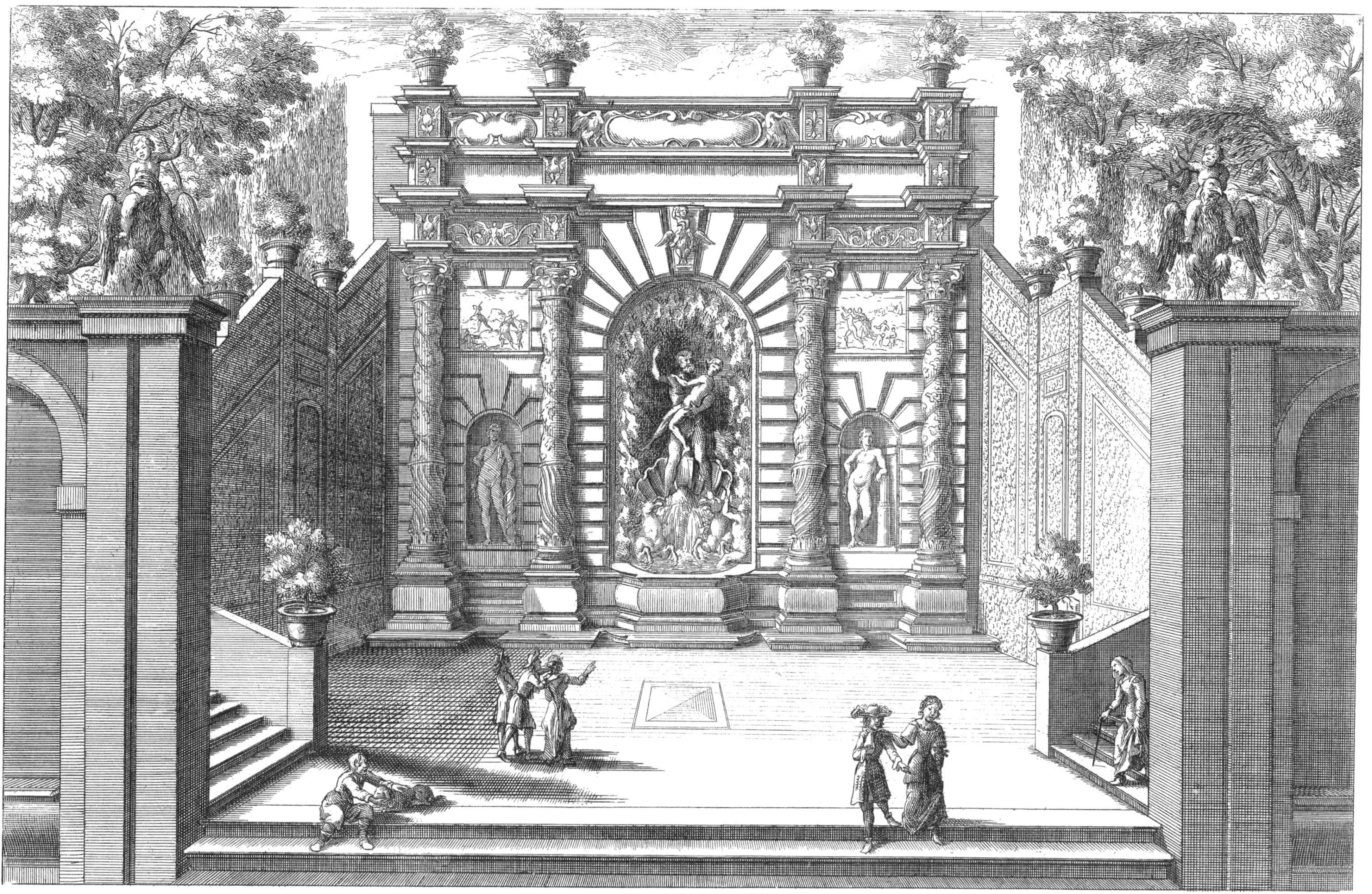

FONTANA DI PROSERPINA CONTIGVA À QVELLA DELLA CIVETTA NEL GIARDINO ESTENSE IN TIVOLI

FOUNTAIN OF PROSERPINA NEXT TO THE FOUNTAIN OF THE OWL IN THE GARDEN OF THE VILLA D'ESTE IN TIVOLI.

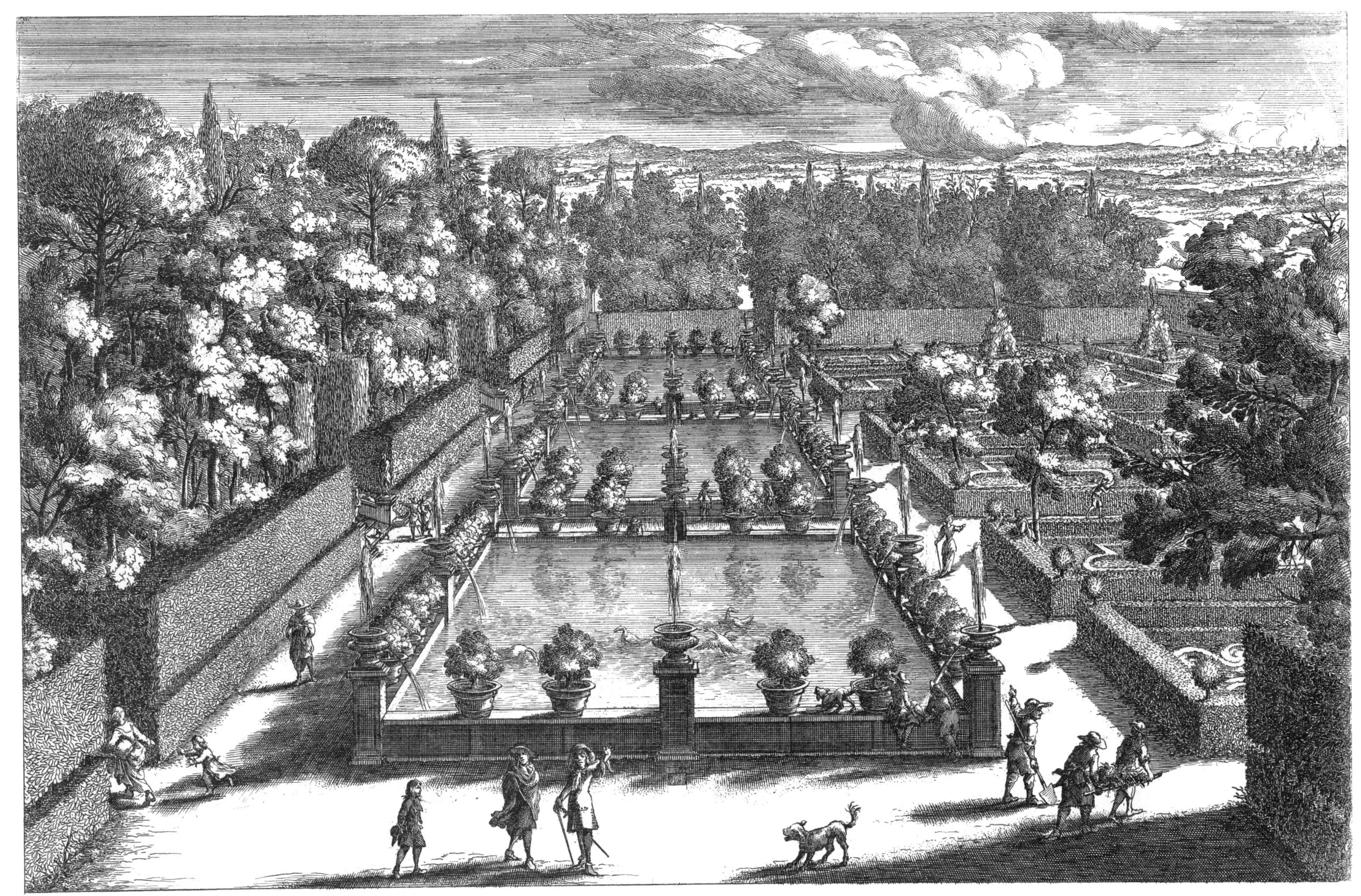

VIEW OF THE FISHPONDS AND WATERWORKS ON THE GARDEN LEVEL.

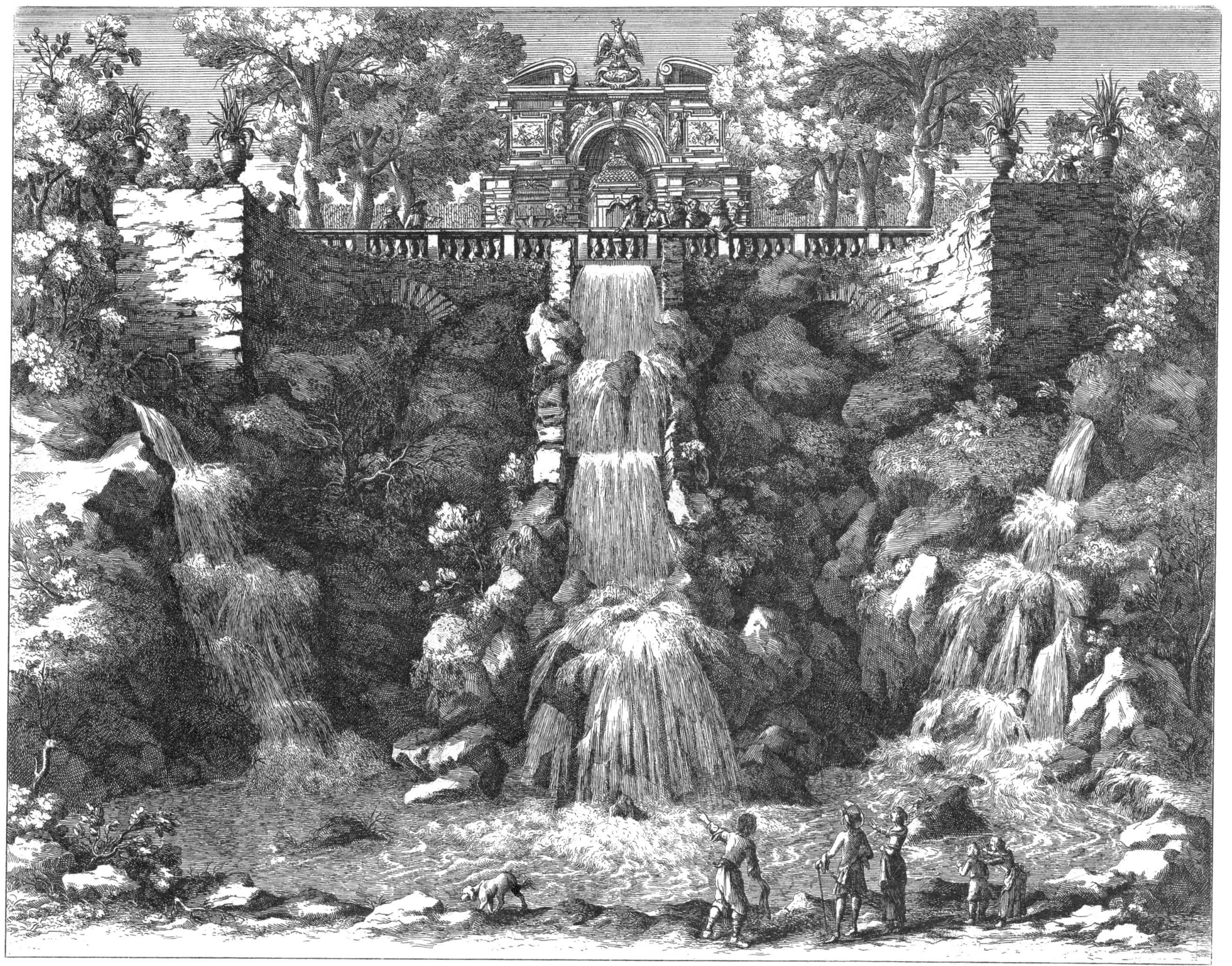

VEDVTA DELLA CASCATA SOTTO L'ORGANO NEL PIANO DEL GIARDINO
VIEW OF THE WATERFALL BENEATH THE ORGAN ON THE GARDEN LEVEL.

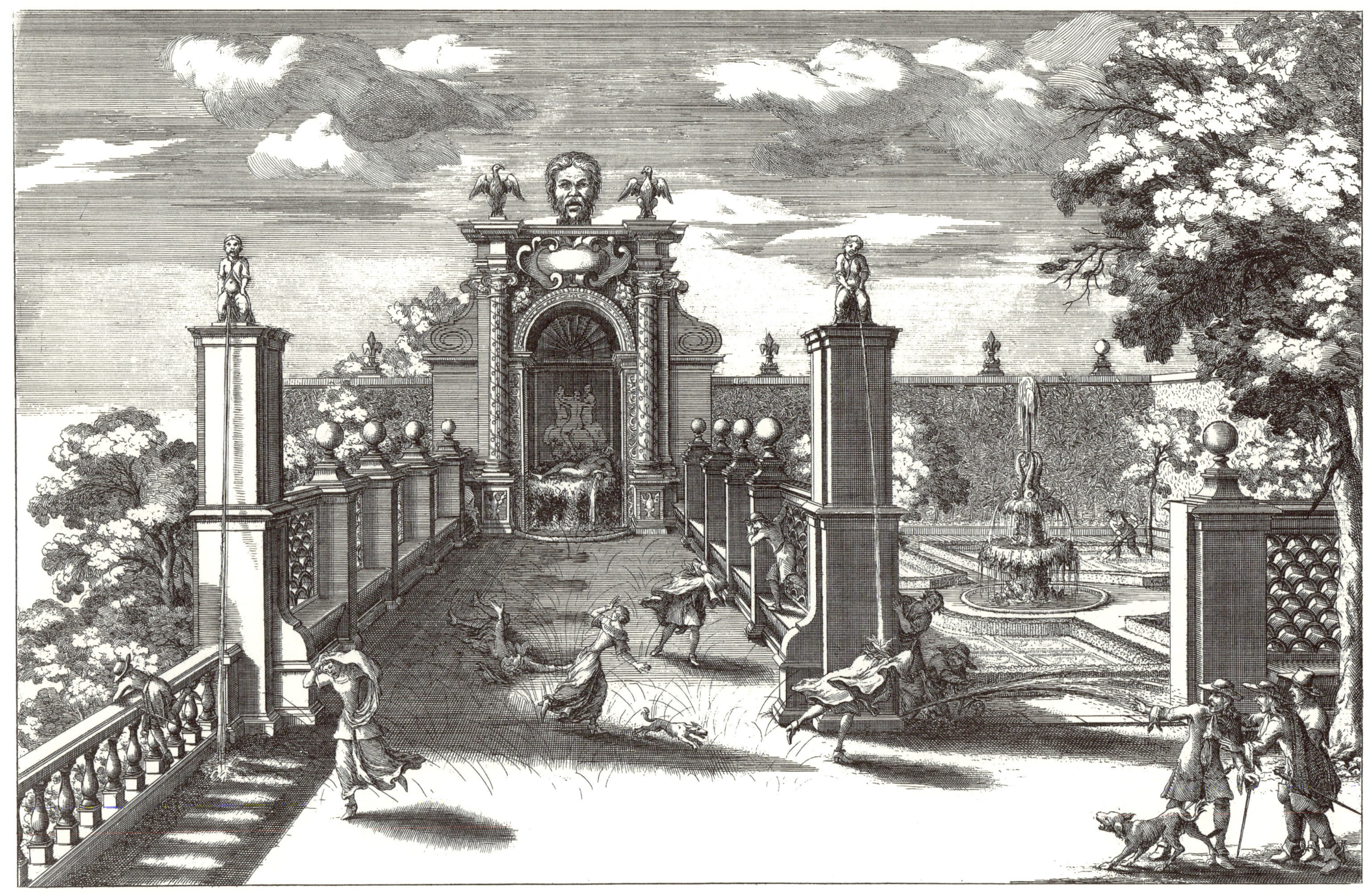

FONTANA DI VENERE POSTA NEL PIANO DELL' ORGANO

FOUNTAIN OF VENUS, LOCATED ON THE LEVEL OF THE ORGAN.

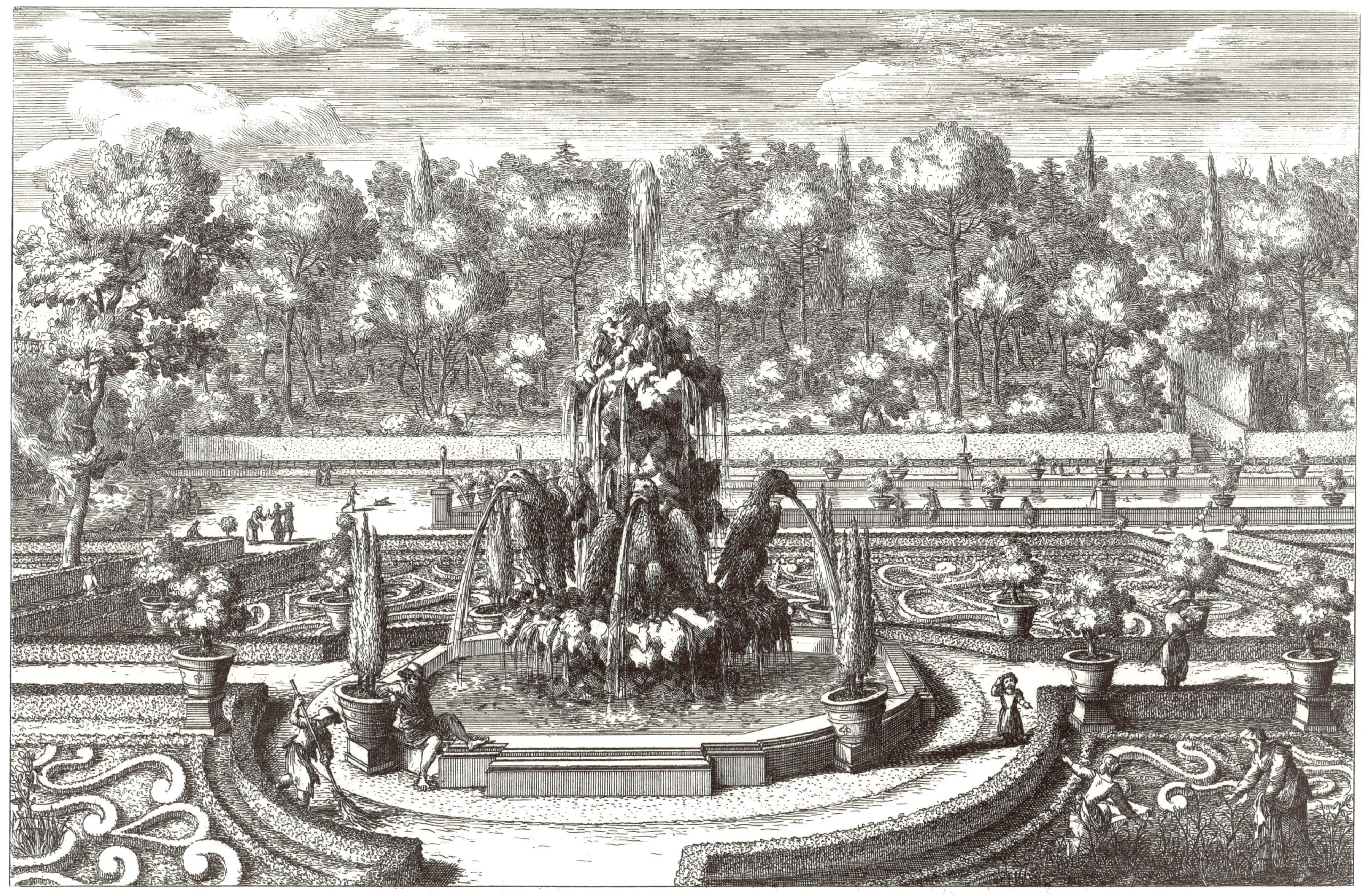

FONTANA DELL' AQVILE ESTENSI POSTA NELLI SPARTIMENTI DEL PIANO DEL GIARDINO

FOUNTAIN OF THE ESTE EAGLES, LOCATED IN THE PARTITIONS OF THE GARDEN.

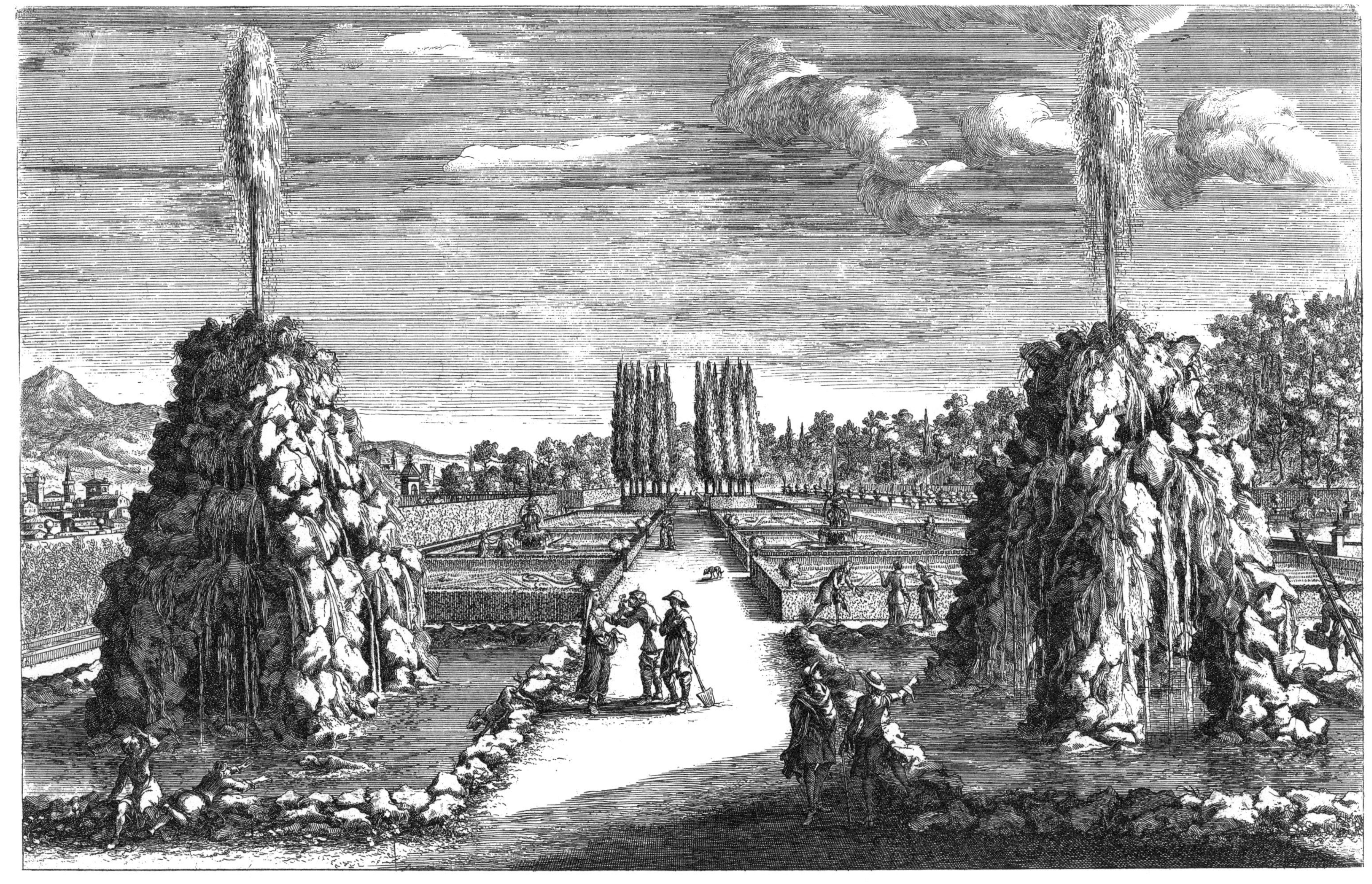

FONTANA DE SCOGLI TRÀ L'ALTRE DVE DE CIGNI, E DE CIPRESSI TRA LI SPARTIMENTI DEL GIARDINO

FOUNTAIN OF THE ROCKS, BETWEEN THE TWIN FOUNTAINS OF THE SWANS, AND CYPRESSES IN THE PARTITIONS OF THE GARDEN.

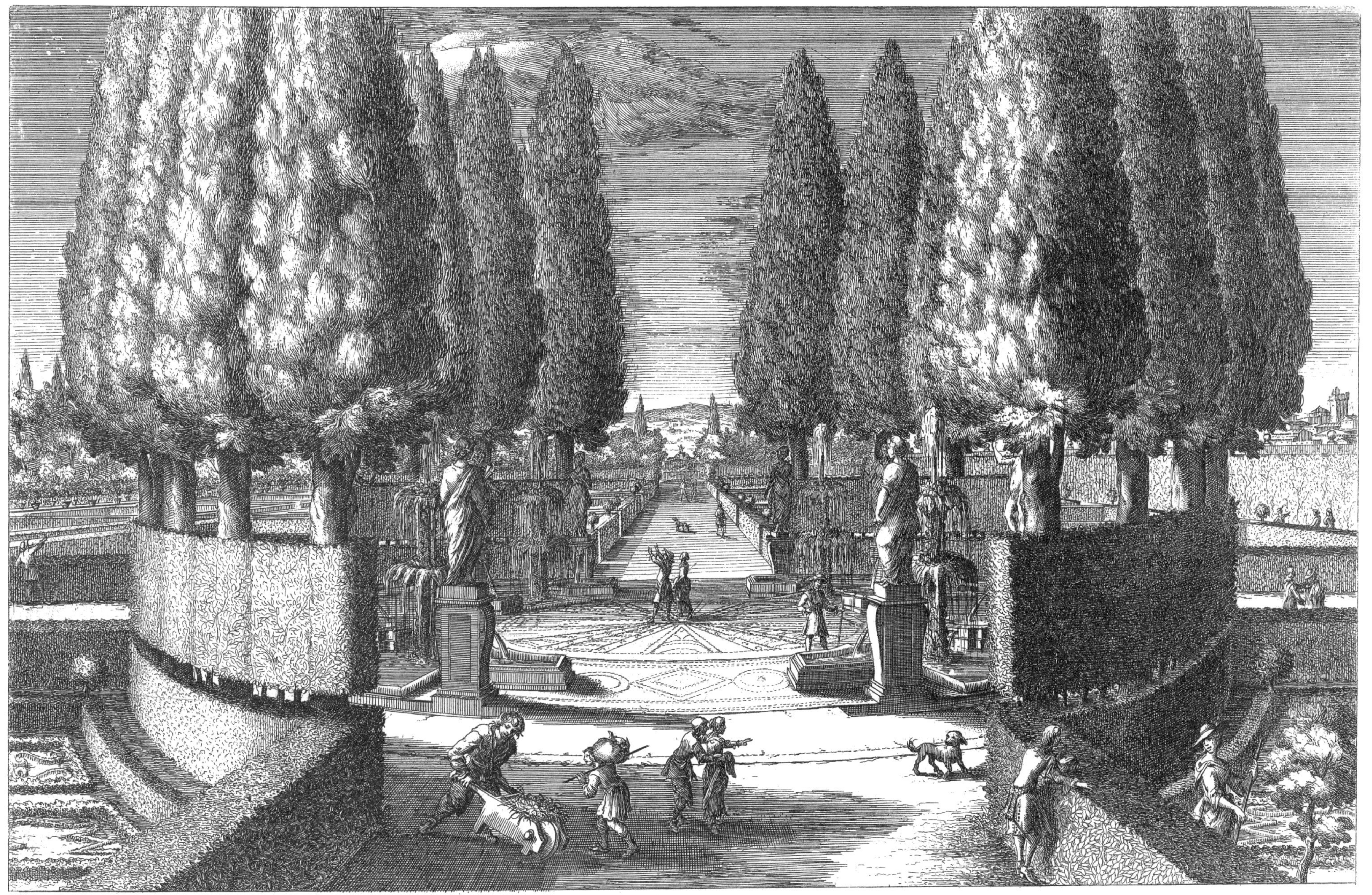

TEATRO DE CIPRESSI CON DODICI SORGIVI D'ACQVA, E CON OTTO STATVE DELL'ARTI LIBERALI NEL PIANO DEL GIARDINO

THE CYPRESS ROTUNDA, WITH TWELVE WATER SPRINGS AND EIGHT STATUES OF THE LIBERAL ARTS, ON THE GARDEN LEVEL.

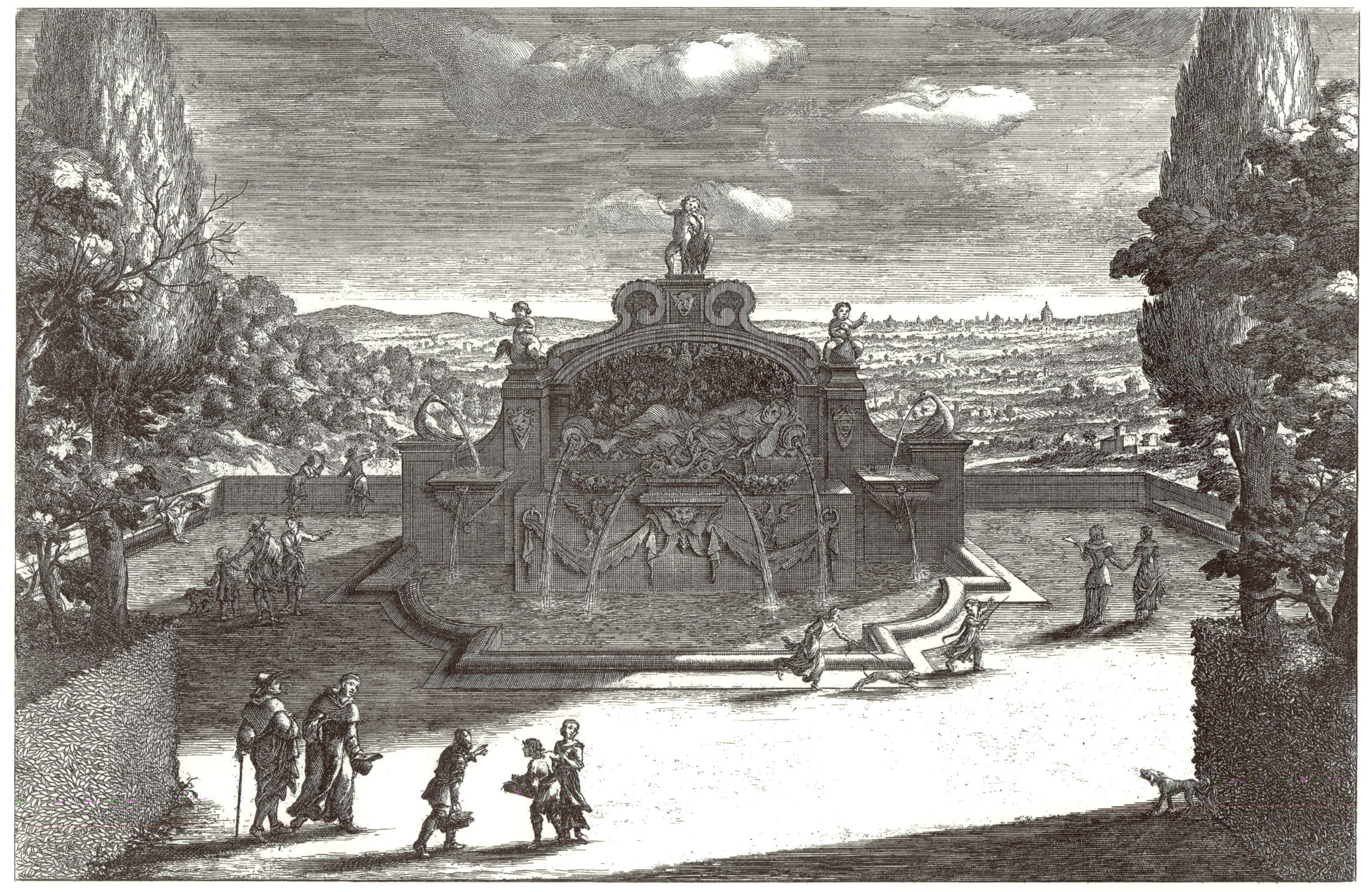

FOUNTAIN OF THE SWANS, WITH STATUE OF A SLEEPING NYMPH, ON THE GARDEN LEVEL.

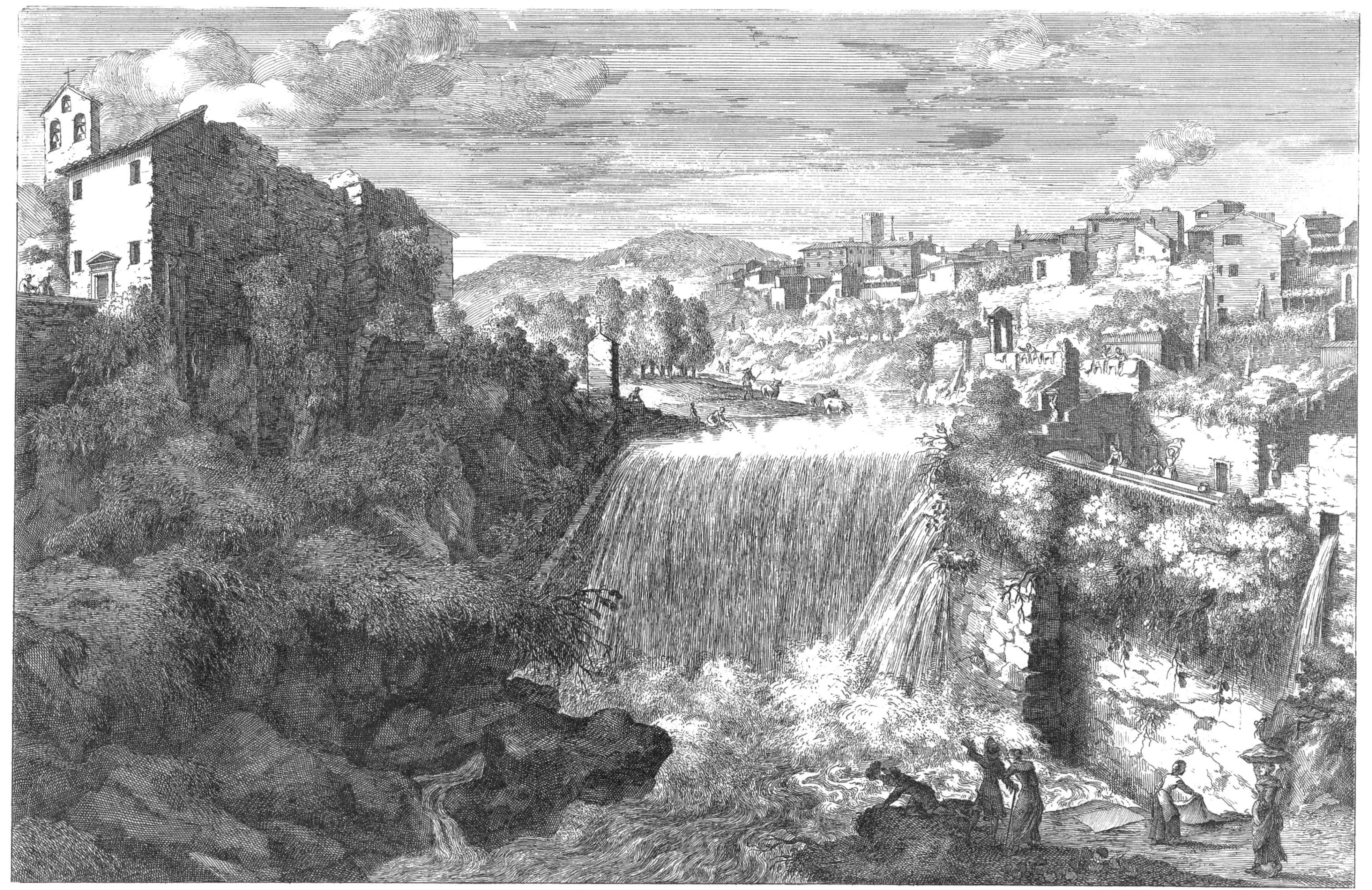

VEDVTA DELLA CASCATA PRINCIPALE DEL FIVME ANIENE NELLA CITTA DI TIVOLI

VIEW OF THE MAIN WATERFALL OF THE ANIENE RIVER IN THE CITY OF TIVOLI.

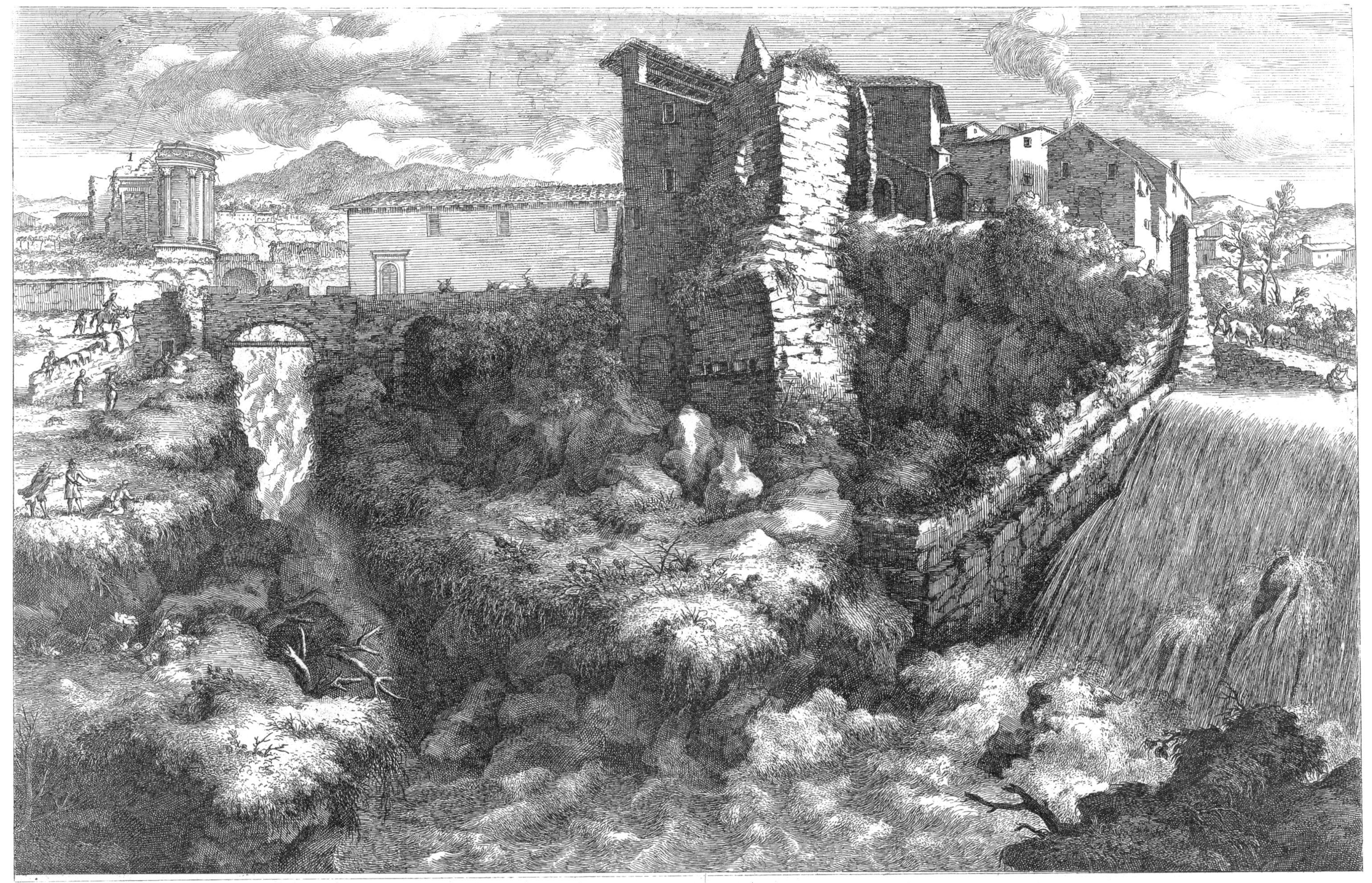

VEDVTA PER FIANCO DELLA CASCATA PRINCIPALE DEL FIVME ANIENE IN TIVOLI

SIDE VIEW OF THE MAIN WATERFALL OF THE ANIENE RIVER IN TIVOLI.